The
Body
Can
Speak

The Body Can Speak

Essays on Creative Movement Education with Emphasis on Dance and Drama

EDITED BY ANNELISE MERTZ

With a Foreword by Joseph Roach

Southern Illinois University Press
Carbondale and Edwardsville

05 04 03 02   4 3 2 1

Library of Congress Cataloging-in-Publication Data

The body can speak : essays on creative movement edu-
cation with emphasis on dance and drama / edited by
Annelise Mertz ; with a foreword by Joseph Roach.
    p. cm.
    Includes bibliographical references.
    1. Dance—Study and teaching. 2. Movement
education. I. Mertz, Annelise.
GV1589 .B63 2002
792.8'071—dc21
                          2001049021
ISBN 0-8093-2418-0 (alk. paper)
ISBN 0-8093-2419-9 (pbk. : alk. paper)

Printed on recycled paper. ✿

To Nik

(Alwin Nikolais), a most innovative
teacher and choreographer, whose philosophical and pedagogical insight have
extended the vision of dance as an art

Alwin Nikolais, founder and former director of the Alwin Nikolais Dance Company,
teaching a master class at Washington University, St. Louis. Photograph by Peter
Zimmerman, Washington University Photographic Service.

Contents

Illustrations

Alwin Nikolais teaching a master class at Washington University *page v*

Following page 44

Michael Ballard and Scott Loebl in *Calligraph for Martyrs*
Ballard and Loebl in *Calligraph for Martyrs*
Amy Schactman in her own solo dance
Ruth Füglistaller performing her own compositional study
Washington University dance student performing her own compositional
     study titled "Shape"
Annelise Mertz teaching a class in modern dance
Annelise Mertz and Murray Louis conversing in the dance studio
Gale Ormiston performing "The Navy Blue Ghost" from the suite *Façade*
Scott Loebl, Michael Ballard, and Gale Ormiston in "Ceremonial Rites
     (The Men)"
Ballard in "Ceremonial Rites (The Men)"
"Ceremonial Rites (The Women)"
Sara Shelton in "The Wonderful Widow of 18 Springs"
Shelton in "The Wonderful Widow of 18 Springs"
Jumay Chu in "Youkali"
"Under the Roof" at the Space Place
"Above the Roof" at the Space Place
"Building Spaces" at the Space Place

Following page 100

G. Hoffman Soto in his own solo dance
Dorothy M. Vislocky teaching a class
Shirley Ririe in her own solo dance
Michael Hoeye and other former Washington University dance students
     in their own group composition
Carol North and other members of the Metro Theater Company in
     Mud Weavings

ix

Foreword

"Ballet is the art of *position*," Erick Hawkins once said, by way of insisting on what he saw as a fundamental distinction between rival forms, whereas "dance," by which he meant the network of movement styles, choreographic traditions, and teaching methods most of us think of as modern dance, "is the art of *transition*." An erstwhile balletomane, I deepened my appreciation of the aesthetics of "the art of transition" during my years of association with Annelise Mertz at Washington University in St. Louis, 1982–87. On the occasion created by this collection of essays by her fellow artists, colleagues, and former students—a sampling of ideas suggestive but far from exhaustive of the work of a lifetime—I want to preface what follows with a brief consideration of the implications of the word *transition*. The dictionary says that it is cognate to *transit* and that it means, narrowly, a passage from one place to another or, more broadly, a movement, development, or evolution from one form, state, stage, or style to another. But that is only a beginning.

For the past forty years, Mertz has resided primarily in the state of Missouri, but she is always in a state of transition. (In German, one can say "always already," and that would be apposite in conveying temperamental predisposition as well as continuing activity.) Whether she has been moving between classroom and stage, between choreographic styles, between the university and the community, or between the music of William Walton and of Scott Joplin, she has always already performed her transitions kinesthetically. The kinesthetic is composed of two equal and interrelated parts, body and soul. Physically, Mertz is never still. Spiritually, she is never satisfied.

In any effort to convey in words what movement can mean or how it can mean, flesh and spirit, body and mind, *psyche* and *soma* naturally come up together in the same breath, so to speak. The phrase that might serve as the motto of Mertz's career as a dancer, teacher, and choreographer—"the body can speak"—also provides an appropriate inspiration for the essays collected here. But no one should suppose that the uneducated body is naturally eloquent. There are at least two ways in which it can fall short of truly articulate speech.

On the one hand, the spirit may be willing, but the flesh is tongue-tied. Contributor Murray Louis, a frequent guest of the Washington University Edison Theater and Dance Department and a charming ironist in the master class, was fond of asking students during warm ups: "Did you take your turnout pills this morning?" In his subtle way, he might possibly have been hinting that they were in no position to make transitions. More generally, he might have been suggesting that in some human endeavors, dance especially, there are no quick and easy physical shortcuts between point A and point B.

On the other hand, sometimes the flesh may be ready, but the spirit is weak. In the body without ideas, however supple and swift, the transitions will mostly be from point A directly to point A. The phrase that I remember best from Mertz's discussions of dance was "the quality of the movement." This was always spoken with gestures that employed different muscle groups in different sequences depending on—and profoundly expressive of—the different aesthetic ideas behind the movement. I learned from watching her closely for five years how the quality of the movement in a choreography by Limon differed from that in a piece by Nikolais. I learned that it was not only because they (and their dancers) had different bodies, although that is no trivial matter, but also because they had different ideas. Different qualities of movement represent different, often radically different, ways of getting from point A to point B.

What the essays collected here attempt to do is translate into words what bodies express with no words (or very few). This requires at once an aesthetic of movement (a *kine* or "movement" plus *aesthetic* equals *kinesthetic*) and a pedagogy of movement. It must be both and not one or the other, because the kinesthetic sense, while it exists in everyone to some extent, must be cultivated and nurtured. It requires at least as much dedication as visual artists devote to training their eyes and musicians their ears. People know, for instance, when they are waving their arms above their heads, even in the dark. But it is another matter entirely for someone (and not just anyone) to appreciate and ultimately to control the expressively beautiful possibilities of these and an infinitude of other corporeal movements. The attainment of such knowledge, which is an expertise in the quality of movement, requires a sensitive imagination, rigorous powers of discrimination, and keen intelligence. To cultivate these, the entire body must be educated. To *educate* means "to draw out." To the student of dance, the difference between being drawn out and being turned out is the difference between being educated and being trained. To be educated in this sense, to be drawn out, means to experience a transition—a movement, an evolution, a change—between states, between positions. To be educated in this sense is both the gift that Mertz gave to generations of her students and the overarching subject of the essays she has collected in the following pages.

—JOSEPH ROACH
YALE UNIVERSITY

Editor's Preface

When I became a professor emerita at Washington University in St. Louis after thirty-one years of teaching, choreographing, and being the director of dance, a number of people suggested that I should write about my experiences; about how I founded and built the dance division and changed it from being considered physical education for women to becoming part of the performing arts department. These were significant events in the history of dance education in the United States. Dance as an art form is still a fairly new phenomenon in academia. It was only about eighty years ago that dance was first offered at the University of Wisconsin at Madison, thanks to the late Margaret H'Doubler. Dance became part of the school's physical education department because the gymnasium was the only space available at that time that was suitable for teaching dance.

At first, I was quite uncertain about writing my own history. I kept paper clippings but never had the time to write down notes during those busy and hectic years. But then I realized, through my own experience, that dance as an art form was still not fully understood and accepted as an important educational subject in the academic world but rather was looked upon as a sideline for the student's exercise and entertainment. Moreover, dance's ephemeral nature removes it further from the tangible quality of science and other academic subjects. Drama has an advantage because it uses the spoken word and therefore can easily be connected with literature and the printed page. Movement is its secondary medium.

Those thoughts strongly motivated me, and I began to write. During this process, I conceived the idea of devoting an entire book to creative movement education as a counterbalance to our technological and computerized life. I felt that collecting and publishing essays by writers who were professionally involved in different ways with creative movement would be a stimulating and informative venture. It would familiarize the general public with many aspects of movement of the human body, which most people regard as only mechanical. Moreover, a creative approach leads inevitably to dance and drama, in fact to all the arts, through the use of rhythm and dynamics. Movement is the very basis of life. It is also our first language.

As Carolyn Moore argues in her book *Beyond Words,* creative movement education is not an "extracurricular luxury" but is of great importance to human experience and therefore can provide a solid basis for learning: "Educational reformers from Rousseau, through Steiner, to Dewey argued that movement education is essential if children are to develop intellectually in a healthy and natural way." In the context of *The Body Can Speak*, I would add *creative* movement education.

I hope this book will help provide new insight into this subject and that it will reach many school administrators, educators, and parents. If dance is taught as a creative art—not as routine nor as commercial entertainment—it completes artistic and physical education for children (both boys and girls). This is *education* in the best sense of the word. Apart from dance, there is no other subject from which such a double value is derived. The fact that so few public and private schools have seen this has always amazed me. Ironically, dance is one of the most neglected subjects in our schools today.

Though *The Body Can Speak* is not intended to cover the entire range of creative movement experience, it is comprehensive enough to give the reader a better understanding of its importance in education and life.

There is more to learning than the three Rs!

Editor's Acknowledgments

First, I would like to extend my appreciation and thanks to all the writers who made such stimulating and informative contributions to the book. Second, I would like to gratefully acknowledge the following people who gave me valuable advice and support: Lorraine Cuoco, director of the Writer's Center at Washington University (St. Louis); Lisa Eck; Joan Gordon; Marianne Friedrich; Paul Thiel; Eva Mesmer; Gene Rodriguez; Val Safron; Margaret Hill; and Samudra Haddad. Special thanks to Adam Bockhorst for his valuable editing and his ever-ready computer. For photography, I am grateful to the Washington University Photographic Service (including but not limited to Tom Stewart, Mark Wagner, Herb Weitman, Peter Zimmerman, and Richard N. Levine) and to David Henschel, Virginia Robinson, Robert Stevens, Nan Melville, Gail Cissna, Brian Gordon, Coni Beeson, Arthur Elgort, Bibi Stromberg, Robert C. Holt, Nat Tileston, Eric Vigil, and J. Bruce Summers.

Part One
As We See It

Man the individual is the creative personality.
Man as artist must dominate man as political
animal. If he can divert his combative drives, he
may survive.

—YEHUDI MENUHIN

I do not believe that education has any significant relation to the creation of works of art,
but I do believe . . . that the creation of works
of art has the most immediate relation possible
to the education of human beings—not only
their education in the arts but their education
for their lives.

—ARCHIBALD MACLEISH,
Art and the Education Process

1

$\mathcal{A}s \, \mathcal{I} \, \mathcal{S}ee \, \mathcal{I}t$

MURRAY LOUIS

I have always thought of dance as a language: a language that speaks through the human body. How clearly that language will speak depends upon how clearly the body can articulate; for with clearness of articulation, there comes clearness of communication. I have dedicated my life to dance and toward achieving this aesthetic clarity of motion. I have sought as a choreographer to select and arrange movement in a manner that would bring my audience into this motional world, to evoke images and sensations, and by so doing, serve as a link between the outer physical world and the spiritual realm within.

Verbal definitions seem inadequate for so profound a subject as art. I feel that only through experiencing art can we enter that vast, gorgeous panorama of the soul to delight and tremble in this world of the senses. To do this, dancers as artists must undertake a particular training, a training that will strip them of their pedestrian limitations and prepare them to reveal the inner life through all the means that comprise the art of dancing.

Art is not nature. It is, however, humanity's way of making a new nature. Humanity does not have millenniums on earth to do its work as nature does. Human beings are rushed through life all too quickly; consequently, they must create their beauty just as quickly.

Beauty is essential to the chemistry of inner fulfillment, and in order to complete itself before it passes on, humankind has, out of necessity, been urged to produce its own beauty artificially. It is at this point that artists appear, and through the selection of materials and under the guidance of an inner judgment, they transform these materials and create a new nature, a humanly constructed naturalism called art. The artist-dancer transmits this new naturalism to the viewer with all the artistry he or she can muster so that the audience can more readily absorb and digest this nourishment for the soul.

When I compose, perform, and teach, I work very directly from creation, to performance, to communication. This thread is fired by a passion, an urgency, and an immediacy called performance. Performance is the cauldron wherein magic, imagery, and the unknown are fused to intoxicate the senses of the audience. But before magic can be created, even the wisest sorcerers must consult their recipes. Once they have determined their ingredients, as with the greatest chefs, they throw the book away and create, making new life appear where none existed before.

There are certain ingredients with which creators must be familiar. These are the principles that comprise the craft of their art. The dancer and choreographer must also acquire certain skills in order to reveal their art. The audience, too, must know their role before they can participate. They must come with open receptivity to what is placed before them.

The vocabulary of abstraction that the dancer and the choreographer use begins with their instrument, the *body*. The body is, in a sense, an orchestra composed of various instruments: arms, legs, head, and torso. They can be played in solo fashion or in various combinations. The dancer works very hard to develop the widest possible range of flexibility and expression in all of these parts.

The *space* surrounding dancers becomes their canvas. They can draw upon it and define it in many ways. The space inside their bodies allows them to give texture and quality to movement. The *time* they employ can range from the pulse of the heartbeat, to the most exacting syncopations, to the denial of time altogether. The manner in which they shape their bodies has the range and freedom that a sculptor employs. There are also *energy* and *dynamics,* and imbuing all is *kinetics,* the excitement that sends motional sensation directly into the viewer's neuromuscular system. All of these can be mixed in any fashion to allow the choreographer a new and different vocabulary for each dance. The dancers, meanwhile, must learn and be able to perform all of these principles as well as develop other skills. *Motional transitions,* for example, are those minuscule attachments that join one movement to another and that allow for the special piquancy dancers bring to their roles.

I communicate my dances through abstraction. I do not generally create story-ballets or interpret characters. In order to communicate these abstractions, I use the language of motion, which I hope my audience can identify and read, not as a narrative but as a series of sensory stimulations. In the art of dance, choreography must occur within a specific time, bounded by the curtain's rising and its fall. In addition, abstractionists must use a nonverbal vocabulary that is not easy to grasp in one viewing. But what they do have, which is much envied by writers and painters, is that wonderful, immediate contact with their audience: the live performance and the power inherent in that contact.

Constantly, there is the question, "What is the purpose of art?" If I may paraphrase the question, I would ask, "Who is the purpose of art?" For me, that purpose is the audience, the public who in the large sense is humankind. The choreographer creates the art, and the performer communicates it to the public, but not in the public's own terms, because they already know their terms, and no new growth would evolve; instead, communication exists in the terms of the artist who hopes to lead them to new insights. All living things need stimulants to grow. Stimulants for the senses are part of the artist's challenge. Art is a stimulant for living and for life.

That is how I see it.

2

Moving into Belonging: The Dance of Mother and Child

BECKY ENGLER-HICKS

Movement means life for the human being, from conception to old age. The power to move is one of our most adaptive characteristics, because survival, adaptation, and learning depend upon effective, creative movement interaction with the environment. The vigorous dance of sperm and egg initially starts the creation of human life, followed by the very active process of cell division and growth. As life progresses, movement experiencing ensures the operation and the functioning of the subsystems of the body and provides both a means of contact with self, others, and objects and the means for revision of behavior from motor feedback. It is very important to have a variety of motor experiences early in life to foster the growth of the human body, the development of the muscular-skeletal systems, and the learning of motor coordination. This is why as a dance-movement therapist I use movement as a powerful and important learning and intervention tool. My specialty is working with parents and their babies up to two years old and with mothers with babies in utero. The purpose of my Baby Bright classes is to provide fundamental interactive infant stimulation. Movement classes are designed to strengthen each child's physical, cognitive, and emotional growth and to give parents tools to help stimulate their child's intelligence and to regulate emotional well-being.

Unfortunately, most parents and educators do not know about the critical role that movement plays in the overall growth and development of the human being. I work with the very youngest of people, because my clinical experience has shown me that the most critical period for the growth of a child's intelligence occurs from conception to age three. Creative movement experiencing helps to build circuitry into the brain. A *Time Magazine* "Special Report" (February 7, 1997) put it this way: "Before and after birth, the baby's brain cells proliferate wildly, making connections that may shape a lifetime of experience and further the child's learning potential."

In the womb, the baby's body is moving continuously. Adaptation to the womb depends upon the positive flow of energy and nutrients through the placenta to the child. During pregnancy, the mother's perception of her environment is also chemically communicated to the fetus, which also feels and responds to her maternal emotions of fear, anger, and love. Parents greatly benefit from prenatal education to become aware of how their actions, attitudes, and thoughts influence the physical and psychological environment of the womb. Mother and child are fundamentally intertwined and need to be supported during pregnancy and birth and after birth. It is important for each child to receive positive imprinting of feelings and memories without trauma.

After birth, the newborn is again constantly in motion: breathing, sucking at the breast, crying, groping, kicking arms and legs. Instinctively, the baby tries out the various movements inherited in utero. For example, the reflex that makes the baby kick is already there in the womb, and it is there in all vertebrates. The reflex is self-sufficient, but it sets the stage for more elaborate movements, which have to be practiced to become automatic. If you put a baby down, it moves, because it is a self-centered motion system. The baby's whole body moves out to its environment to receive tactile, auditory, visual, and kinesthetic feedback. These acts allow it to receive a good supply of vital energy for growth. Movement acts as a growth stimulant. The body with its movement is continually changing in response to how it is used, how often, and under what circumstances. The baby builds muscular strength when it moves, which allows for the development of eye-hand coordination, the learning of locomotor skills, and the achieving of upright posture.

Since learning revolves around children's motor input, it is imperative that parents learn how to assist their children's learning potential. The baby and toddler need daily doses of respect, love, attention, and physical handling with a variety of other stimulation to make physical and conceptual progress. Babies are totally dependent on their primary caregivers to provide them with quality interaction at an appropriate developmental level. Also, parents want the latest educational information to do their best jobs. The dynamics of the parent-infant interaction is one of the most important foundations on which children develop a clear sense of themselves to develop self-esteem.

It is important that parents enjoy playing with their babies. They can teach active ways of responding to stimuli through modeling, imitation, and reinforcement of motor action. In my Baby Bright classes, parents of newborns are encouraged to actively hold, hug, touch, snuggle, rub, massage, and kiss their babies. Loving the baby physically with gentle stroking, rocking, and cradling movements builds basic trust. Moving together in synchrony when dancing, swaying, and rocking is soothing to the baby as parent and infant match rhythms. This encourages the bonding process through the experience of mutual movement attunement. Also, parents and caretakers need to respond quickly and directly to the baby's cues, using direct eye contact, actions, and sounds. Imitating the child's facial expressions, noises, and body postures encourages the child's awareness of self and body parts as well as encourages communication. Paying close attention and verbalizing what a child might be feeling gives feedback about the child's internal sensations and feelings. In addition, it helps to focus the child's attention, enabling it to learn.

Neurological research in the 1990s revealed that there is a clear window of opportunity during the first two years of life for the development of motor skills. Movement patterning is obviously reinforced through practice and repetition. Babies need to be put down on the floor and encouraged to move their bodies and limbs. They need a safe place with space to move. Learning to roll over, creep, sit, crawl, stand up, and walk help to lay down and consolidate pathways in the brain, which make possible the learning of more complex locomotor skills later on. It is important for parents to understand that movement, with its feedback system, encodes the central nervous system. Obviously, the amount of information that children receive as they move influences the growth and development of the central nervous system. Movement experiencing accurately records in the central nervous system exact reactions, emotions, and responses that children are having to their environment. The first patterned pathways made in the brain and central nervous system are the most powerful because they function as the primary conduits through which later sensory input, motor behavior, emotions, and cognitive patterns will flow. Movement is always enhancing the formation of the child's memories. The implications of this research are enormous. We must begin as early as possible to create emotionally secure and intelligent human beings who are movers. There is a qualitative difference between the children who receive infant stimulation with movement emphasis and those who do not. Great futures begin with a stimulating, moving start!

Creative movement experiencing and creative facilitation are the keys to help babies survive and thrive. Movement patterning is obviously reinforced through practice and repetition, but children must be shown many different ways to use their bodies to express themselves to set a response. An activity that is to be learned thoroughly must be presented and experienced through multisensory experiencing. I always suggest to the parents that they encourage the baby to "move or be moved" on different textures, in different directions, and in a variety of ways with various amounts of force. The individuals who exhibit the widest variation in the force, time, space, flow, and weight patterns of their movement create for themselves an expanded movement behavior style that is flexible to suit their needs. Also, it is important to note that although the attainment of motor skills may not seem very complex, the most highly integrated behaviors are those pertaining to motor coordination. The physicality of movement and its repetition at the right time with appropriate input creates positive behavior changes.

Children and their creative movement expressions are the center of concern when structuring activities for enrichment. The idea is to create problem-solving opportunities where there are many solutions and where the children can easily succeed. The children then feel joyfully motivated to create new movement for themselves to enlarge their movement behavior vocabulary. Then they want to expand their intelligence through self-directed discovery learning. There is less chance of their having a fear of failing. The environment encourages spontaneity and openness. There is excitement about learning and freedom, and there is space to create and express openly, through movement, what they feel, perceive, and sense. There is access to a variety of tools and materials that might stir and excite the imagination. Parents and educators who love and respect their children would do well to provide movement learning to the fetus, the baby, and the toddler. It is truly the gift of knowledge to the child for discovery of the self and for the formation of body-mind structures that foster the child's reaching its full learning potential.

3
Education Through Dance

MARGARET N. H'DOUBLER

If dance is to function again as a vital experience in the lives of our people, it must be the responsibility of our educators. This inclusion of dance in the general education program is the one means of giving free opportunity to all children for experiencing the contributions it can make to their developing personalities and their growing artistic natures.

In considering such a plan, we should be able to answer such questions as these: What do we mean by dance? What are its ultimate values and justifications? Of what importance is creative art activity in the development of the mind? And finally, what is its value for the individual? Such a search into the nature of dance yields a philosophy based on a fundamental belief in the artistic and aesthetic capacities of human nature and in the values of expression through some creative art activity. From this philosophy must be formed a theory that will be an expression of the aims for which dance should work well as a formulation of the underlying principles. An example of such a formulation is the insistence that dance be experienced as an adequate means of expression, so that when the movements of the intellectual, emotional, and spiritual natures are coordinated with the activities of the body, there will result an expression that is vital and dynamic.

To work toward this end, we must build a theory on a knowledge of the structure of the body and the laws of bodily movement. And to appreciate and understand the relation between feeling and action, we must know the psychology of the emotions and the part they play in the urge to expression in movement. This carries us over into the science of dance: the systematized knowledge that tells us how to go to work—and how to adjust our efforts to attain the desired ends. These ends will depend upon the view we hold for art, its social and individual values. Also, we must develop a technique that will result in forms that are in accordance with this artistic tradition.

Revised from Margaret N. H'Doubler, *Dance: A Creative Art Experience.* Copyright © 1957. Reprinted by permission of the University of Wisconsin Press.

No one who understands the relation of the arts to human personality can question their values in education, nor can those who have followed educational science during recent years fail to see that provision for the arts must be made in any adequate educational plan. If we go to one of the first masters of educational theory, Plato, we are told that "the purpose of education is to give to the body and soul all the beauty and all the perfection of which they are capable." This definition of purpose still holds, but today we would qualify Plato's statement in some such manner as that suggested by Spencer in his definition of life as "The conscious adjustment of internal relations to external." Both views, it is clear, focus upon the development and growth of the individual, and both imply self-activity, which we may take as the keynote of current educational speculation.

The higher aim of education today is the development to the fullest extent of the growth of the individual, based upon a scientific understanding of all his or her needs and capacities. In so doing, we try to attune our own thinking to harmonize with students' particular interests, because we realize that in their interests lie the key to their needs and capacities. Education cannot supply individual capacities—these must be inborn—but it can stimulate and aid in their growth; it can assist students by giving them the opportunity to develop themselves.

There are two aspects to education: one, the capacity to take in, to become impressed; the other, the capacity to give out, to express. To receive impressions informs the mind, but to express its reactions to these impressions requires coordination and cooperation of all the mental powers. Power to perceive and to evaluate experience is a high faculty but of little use unless put into execution. Mere perception and comprehension of knowledge are not sufficient for the fullest development of the mind. To know is the essential first step, but it is the expression of what we know that develops character and a sense of values. It is through perception, intuition, feeling, and conception that our personalities assimilate experience and work it up into our own substance and the world of thought, emotion, and will.

Without this metabolism of experience, damage is done to the emerging personality. It is likely to become overburdened and disorganized with undigested and unassimilated information, and inner spontaneity becomes hampered. If dance education is to contribute to this psychic integration, it is essential that students experience movement in forms characteristic of human responses; that they be led, consciously, from the more natural movement types determined by structure to those responses that are variable and individually modifiable and under the control of higher associative processes; and finally, it is essential that they experience and evaluate, as they progress, the accompanying feeling tones of emotional enrichment.

In other words, dance education must be emotional, intellectual, and spiritual, as well as physical, if dance is to contribute to the larger aims of education—the developing of personality through conscious experiencing. It should capitalize every possible resource, selecting and integrating the contributions into a totality.

If we accept the belief in the organized wholeness of human beings, it is evident that the development of their energies must be interdependent. Our emotions and desires need intelligent selection and guidance, and to be carried to their fullest expression, they demand skillful execution.

In such a concept of human development, the body should be considered as the outer aspect of personality, for it is the agent through which we receive impressions from the external world and by which we communicate our meaning. Thus, the body should be given as careful a study and as high a perfection of technique as the associated processes of thought and feeling. The most completely developed persons are the ones who have trained all their powers with equal dignity and consideration in order that they may be physically, intellectually, and emotionally integrated. We may restate the meaning of education as the disciplining and training of our powers and the attainment of skill in execution.

The very nature of the arts makes them especially adapted to this ideal of education, for it is only in art that all the aspects of humanity's complex nature are united in expression. In art, as in reality, the drives are of the emotional nature; when subjected to the restraint and directions of the intellect and executed by the physical, they result in a fusion of all our energies with the focal point centered in the personality.

The place of dance in developing such individual growth is understood if personality is defined as the expressive total of all our physical, emotional, intellectual, and spiritual energies. These energies are in a constant state of reacting to, and being acted upon by, the social order in which we live. Of all the arts, dance is peculiarly suited to such a fulfillment of the personality. It serves all the ends of individual growth; it helps to develop the body; it stimulates the imagination and challenges the intellect; it helps to cultivate an appreciation for beauty; and it deepens and refines the emotional nature.

In the teaching and the studying of dance, we should not be concerned whether or not students develop into professional or recital dancers. The concern should be to develop the power of expression through the study of dance. It may be asked whether the expression of ordinary people is of special interest in the professional art. We go to the works of the greatest artists for the wisdom and beauty and emotion they can communicate to us. But expression, execution, and sharing also belong to general education, and they are needs felt by all normal people.

Too often, the tendency is to center dance education in performance, with the emphasis on technical skill, instead of studying the subject as a whole and using creative motor experience as the basis of instruction. In considering dance as an educational and creative art experience and not as performance, we should take care that students know dance as a special way of reexperiencing aesthetic values discovered in reality. Everyone has within himself or herself the same potentialities as the artist dancer but perhaps to a lesser degree. Everyone has intellect, emotion, spirit, imagination, ability to move, and educable responses. Every normal person is equipped with the power to think, feel, will, and act. Anyone can dance within the limits of his or her capacities. To bring this to the realization of our youth necessitates an approach that is based on these fundamental human capacities. One of the problems is how to keep the creative impulse alive through the maturing years and how to help carry this impulse over into the realities of adult life with heightened power and more enlightened purpose. The basic forces underlying all living forms must be realized as the source of the creative impulse that impels them to expression.

If dance is to realize these educational possibilities, it must take upon itself a form that is suited to them. It should base its movement forms upon the laws of bodily motion, and the study of motion should include movement in all the forms characteristic of human responses. At the same time, its techniques should be simple enough to afford amateur students sufficient mastery of their bodies as their instruments of expression and complex enough to prove interesting and valuable to those who wish to make dance their chosen profession. The rhythmic scope of dance will need to be sufficiently broad to include the varying personal rhythms of the students, and its forms and content will need to be flexible enough to provide opportunity for widely different expressions of widely different individuals.

Although such an approach to dance does not insist on artistic perfection from the professional critic's point of view, it can insist on high amateur standards and, in so doing, build a foundation for the development of a keen artistic integrity and appreciation. From such a background of study will arise those who are destined by original endowment to become our artist dancers. Our first concern is to teach boys and girls and men and women by means of dance, to teach dance as an experience that contributes to a philosophy and a scheme of living.

It is to be expected that not everyone will be a great dancer and that dancing, of course, will be experienced as a complete art form more by some than by others; but just as all children have a right to a box of crayons and some instruction in the fundamental principles of drawing and in the use of color, whether or not they have any chance of becoming professional artists, so all children have a right to know how to achieve control of their bodies in order that they may use it to the limit of their abilities for the expression of their own reactions to life. Even if they can never carry their efforts far enough to realize dance in its highest forms, they may experience the sheer joy of the rhythmic sense of free, controlled, and expressive movement and through this know an addition to life to which every human being is entitled. If the interest in giving instruction in dance is only to produce dancers, dance as a creative and pleasurable art experience, possible to all, is doomed. It is because of concern over this tendency that those who are convinced of the value of dance are striving to restore to society a dance that is creative, expressive, communicable, and social, a dance form that in every way will qualify as art.

4
The Common Aesthetic

RUTH GRAUERT

Bearnstow, a summer arts camp in central Maine, offers in its Intensive Arts Program four disciplines with a period in each for five days. During our day camp program, each art discipline is offered for ten classes over a span of two weeks. Each of the disciplines deals with a distinct energy. Music is concerned with the formulation of sound, visual arts with light, dance with motion, poetry with mind; and theater is all of these, combining sound, light, motion, and mind.

As simplistic or as recondite as these basic definitions seem, they may prove to be the only ones that are universally valid. In common, the separate disciplines share those elements that we have come to believe define our universe: *time* as duration and reiteration, *space* as volume and linear projection, *energy* as continuum and change.

The held note of the horn in which we reach the stars, the measured pace of iambic pentameter that leads us gently to know the unknowable, the supported leap of the ballerina that takes our breath with it, the deep perspective that guides us to new worlds: It is the time, space, and energy contained in these moments that make our trips possible. In its own province, each of these elements is shaped by the same modifiers in all their variations and contrasts, from monstrous to minute. There is hard and soft, bright and dull, heavy and light, strong and weak, loud and quiet, fast and slow, large and small . . . are there more?

Shelley cries, "I weep for Adonais—he is dead!" Do you hear music sounding its eternal slowness? Do you see colors deepening? Does your body sink? On Cummings's coastal plain "the hours rise up putting off stars." Is not sound growing and punctuating? Does not the light become clear? Do you not sit up? Have you seen Brancusi's sculpture *Bird in Flight*, that simple shaft of gleam? Can you say you did not soar? And what did you hear when you looked on Picasso's *Guernica*? Do you not know the scream of horror? You hear "Here's looking at you, kid," and where are you in place and time? What do you hear and smell and feel? There is only one connection between us and art, and that is our humanity. Our participation in life must lead us to art, and art in turn will lead us to what we truly are.

Say "The Mississippi is a long, long river." Vary the pace and the cadence. Speak loudly, then softly, full voice, falsetto. Draw the river long or wide. Change the color as it goes. Stomp your feet or clap your hands as the river tells you to. From this simple "poetry," we have gained music and picture and dance and theater.

Art is *not* the skills we have. Music is *not* the knowledge of middle C and high G. Visual art is *not* knowing how to mix blue and yellow. Dance is *not* distinguishing between a hop and a jump. Poetry is *not* the spelling of the word. Clap your hands, and you have both music and dance. Put on colored gloves, and you have visual art. Open your mouth with accompanying words, and you have poetry and theater.

Of course, art is not this easy. But this is where it starts—with the realization that each of us as human beings, regardless of learned skills, are capable of bringing into palpable structure that which may be called art. First, we learn to tap the source of art (ourselves), and then with discriminative application of the elements, we refine what we regurgitate. The essential skill is what we teach ourselves as we proceed from tapping to tapping.

Art is not difficult. Dance is as simple as sticking out your tongue, thumbing your nose, stamping your foot, bending your back, turning your head. Music is as easy as clapping your hands, clicking your tongue, slapping your chest, sustaining your whistle. Visual art is as casual as choosing the color of your socks, placing your plate on the table, making your mark in the sand. Poetry is as direct as speaking your mind, demanding candy, saying "Hi." And perhaps having a tantrum is all the arts put together: sound and motion and words; and you are bound to turn *red*, and of course, with a tantrum there is contrast, so we have theater.

Art is communication. As we learn to make our own, we learn to listen, feel, and know what others wish to tell us. In this way, we truly live many lives, knowing others as we know ourselves, even those from whom we are separated by time or space, centuries or culture. Art is the greatest adventure of all, for with it we can go from the center of the earth to the farthest star, from the beginning of time to time's collapse. We can know beings long gone or far away, feel their feelings, see their sights, hear their songs. Art is one village in all of time, so let's get with it and enter that village gate.

In detailing this theory as the source of our art, we need to acknowledge Alwin Nikolais, who set fire to our being and then gave us the freedom to stand on our own.

We view the relationship of the arts and the earth simply as fundamental. All of us as human beings certainly interact with our environment on a daily basis. To pull from this interaction an aesthetic product is what most arts are all about. To bring forth a statement formed with motion, sound, color, and words can hit the human perception in all its senses. Over and above all this is the fact that our arts are laden with conventions, some of current pertinence, some not. These conventions may support or burden the creative perception. One way to clear the nasal passages, so to speak, is to go back to home base— to our eyes and ears, our noses and skin, all our senses. Of course, this has been a common practice for artists; painters have done so over the ages. Why not all of us? What Bearnstow's Intensive Art Program offers is a time to work our craft in a place of clear beauty, a time to find rhythms in wind and rocks, colors in trees and skies, words in the sighs of night, sounds in the growing day. And leisure to touch oneself.

5
Art and the Intellect

HAROLD TAYLOR

The intellect is usually defined as a separate faculty in human beings: the ability to think about facts and ideas and to put them in order. The intellect is usually contrasted with the emotions, which are thought to distort facts and ideas, or contrasted with the imagination, which departs from facts. As a result, it is often assumed that intellectuals are people who think, who have the facts and the ideas, and that the rest of society is composed of nonintellectuals and anti-intellectuals who don't think. This is, of course, not the case, and it is possible to be an intellectual and not be intelligent or to be a nonintellectual and think very well.

It is also assumed that there are basic differences between science and art, between scientists and artists. It is assumed that scientists are rational, objective, abstract, and concerned with the intellect and with reducing everything to a formula; and that artists, on the other hand, are temperamental, subjective, irrational, and concerned with the expression of the emotions. But we all know temperamental, irrational scientists and abstract, cold-blooded artists. We know, too, that there is a body of knowledge in art. There are as many facts and ideas in art as there are in any other field, and there are as many kinds of art as there are ideas—abstract or concrete, classical, romantic, organized, unorganized, expressionist, surrealist, intuitive, intellectual, sublime, ridiculous, boring, exciting, and dozens of others. The trouble lies in thinking about art the way most people think about the intellect. It is not what they think it is.

This would not be quite so serious a matter if it were not taken so seriously, especially by educators and those who urge their views upon educators—that is, I suppose, the rest of humankind. If thinking is an activity that takes place in a separate faculty of the intellect, and if the aim of education is to teach people to think, it is therefore natural to assume that education should train the intellect through the academic disciplines. These disciplines are considered to be the subject matter for intellectual training, and they consist of facts and ideas from the major fields of human knowledge, organized in such a way that the intellect can deal with them, that is to say, in abstract, conceptual, logical terms. It is assumed that learning to think is a matter of learning to recognize and understand these concepts. Educational programs in school and college are therefore arranged with this idea in mind, and when demands for the improvement of education are made, they usually consist of demands for more academic material to be covered and more academic discipline of this kind to be imposed. It is a call for more organization, not for more learning. One of the most unfortunate results of this misunderstanding of the nature of the intellect is that the practice of the arts and the creative arts themselves are too often excluded from the regular curriculum of school and college or are given such a minor role in the educational process that they are unable to make the intellectual contribution of which they are supremely capable.

When human knowledge is considered to be an organized body of facts and ideas, it seems to possess an independent reality, to exist by itself in time and space. In fact, it does not. Knowledge does not exist until it is known by someone. It merely seems to exist because it can be recorded in symbols, words, and numbers. Few educators realize that dance, music, painting, design, and sculpture are forms of knowledge even though they do not express themselves in words. These arts can be talked about, and facts can be assembled to describe their history and their characteristics, which is what most educators want to do with them, but that is not the most important thing about them as far as education is concerned. The important thing is the experience, the discipline and the joy they give to those who engage in them and learn to value them. Such experience provides knowledge of a kind different from the knowledge expressed in words but possessing a special kind of value. Only after the experience is gained is there any point in talking or writing about it, and even then, the purpose in talking and writing about that experience is to lead on to further experience and further understanding.

In spite of the truth of this idea, which seems so obvious, most colleges and schools allow their students to learn about the arts only through slides, lectures, textbooks, histories, and appreciation courses and not to engage in the arts themselves. That is, except in nursery schools, in elementary schools, and in colleges preparing students for teaching in nursery and elementary schools, where presumably it does not matter.

I wish to present the view that teaching people to think is not merely a question of training their intellects through the study of organized bodies of fact.

This approach may very well teach them not to think but to memorize and accept what they are given, since all the work has been done for them, and there is really nothing left to think about. The main problem is to teach people not only to think but to think for themselves and to organize their own bodies of knowledge and experience. The intellect is not a separate faculty. It is an activity of the whole organism, an activity that begins in the senses with direct experience of facts, events, and ideas, and it involves the emotions. The activity of thinking begins when individuals are impelled to think by the presence of questions that they require answers for. They begin thinking when they are involved in experiences that require them to place these experiences in some kind of order. Until the individuals become sensitive to experience and to ideas, until these things mean something to them personally, or to put it differently, until they become conscious of the world around them and wish to understand it, they are not able to think creatively either about themselves or about their world. Their sensibilities, their values, and their attitudes are the keys to their intellect. It is for this reason that the arts, since they have most directly to do with the development of sensibility, are an essential component of all learning, including scientific learning.

If we take this view, then education is itself an art, the art of teaching attitudes and values. An intellectual life begins for students when their life includes intellectual interests of their own choosing, when they put forth intellectual effort, that is, when they commit themselves to learning because they want to. Once an attitude is established, students begin to organize their own bodies of knowledge and to conduct their own education. In this process, the teacher becomes an artist in the same sense that a writer or a painter is an artist. The teacher and the artist both express in their work their own attitude to life and the way they see things, thus evoking a response in students or in observers. But the information being conveyed or the subject matter used by the painter or the teacher, although it may be important in itself and may be interesting in its own right, is primarily a vehicle for an attitude being communicated.

For example, one of the things we wish to create in students is an attitude to learning. We want our students to love learning, to be interested in ideas, to respect deeply the life of the mind. The subject matter through which this respect is reached may be drawn from any field. But only when the attitude is present will there be true learning and true discipline, since without it, the students withhold their real selves and make no serious commitment. This is as true of science as it is of art; abstractions will not come to life until the student breathes life into them.

On the other hand, those who believe that the creative arts are central to education and that the arts contain within themselves an intellectual discipline no less demanding than that of the sciences must be very clear about what they mean and how they propose to apply what they mean. Too often, it is considered enough to condemn the philistines and the dullards who do not understand the arts, to proclaim the unique virtue of art in education, turn as many students as possible loose in the studios and theaters, and hope for the best—that they will express themselves and everything will come out all right.

Cesar Barber of Amherst College spoke recently of the meaning of academic discipline by comparing it with the discipline of religion. The discipline of religion, he said, consists of performing certain rituals—going to church, praying, contemplating, fasting, and reading the Bible, the Koran, or another text—the purpose of which is to become religious. The person becomes religious by undergoing the discipline, and the purpose of the discipline is to enable the person to be religious. Religion is the end, the discipline is the means, and the person willingly and devoutly undergoes a series of acts that he or she wishes to perfect in order to perfect personal awareness of a God, to come closer to that reality. By engaging in these acts in the spirit of commitment, one becomes religious.

The intellectual disciplines and the disciplines of art share this characteristic, and the purpose of their discipline is to achieve an awareness of ideas and values that otherwise would remain unavailable. It is therefore of the utmost importance to be clear that in those forms of education that concern themselves directly with the education of the emotions and with the development of sensibility, there exist appropriate and adequate acts through which the ends may be achieved. It is not enough merely to feel, to express, to enjoy, and to gesture. Ecstasy itself has its own necessary conditions and antecedents.

My plea is for the restoration of the personal element in modern life and in modern education at a time when everything is pushing us into collective states of mind and into the safety of anonymous opinion. We are being pushed into group thinking because many persons are willing to strip themselves of their individuality to become clusters of approved characteristics held in place by a desire to be liked and to be successful. Nor do I mean by the *personal element* the element of self-analysis. I mean the robust assertion of personal belief. American culture has become fascinated by its self-analysis. Its novels are introspective, almost totally concerned with personal questions, with relationships, with personal manners; its theater and poetry have turned to the emotional content of human life and away from the bigger human issues; its social comment has to do with the nature of the American character. We have created a self-absorbed culture just now, concerned with psychological comfort, running for the doctor before we feel the chill. Our intellectuals are more interested in analysis than in construction, more in probing and reporting than in acting. It is a country of committees, surveys, and questionnaires. Whenever an action is proposed or an idea is held, it is first given a test to decide in advance whether the action will be approved or the idea accepted. When anything is suggested, a thousand little people run out to say why it can't be done or how it might fail. I don't know where they come from, but they're there. There is such a deal of peering, peeking, probing, and harassing on all sides that it is a wonder that anything gets done at all.

In the middle of the welter of contemporary obstructions, it is important to remember that education is the means by which students can find their selfhood. It is the way in which students can find out what they believe, the way they can establish standards according to which they will live, the way they can find images of themselves and of their duties. Students must gain a sense of their possibilities and of the range of action they know they can undertake and that they want to undertake. There is, therefore, a double task for students—learning to do something useful for their society and their fellows, and learning to know the range of possible human experience; that is, creating in themselves a rich inner life, stocked with ideas and facts that are their own and that elevate them and release them from ignorance and error.

But to achieve genuine individuality in the modern world, one does not try always to be an individual. Individualism is achieved by trying to be honest with oneself, honest in one's judgments, tastes, and preferences; individualism is an outcome of this effort—it is not its purpose. The trouble is that most kinds of education are devoted to teaching students not how to be themselves but instead how to cover up, how to gain enough knowledge, for example, in a survey course in Western civilization so that no one will ever know that they haven't read any of the authors or that they haven't ever really understood the works of art they were asked to observe. The usual kind of education—that is, the kind that is divided into courses, condensed into textbooks, put out in three lectures a week, tested by examinations, and rewarded by three academic credits a throw—is designed to give answers to questions that nobody asked and to inhibit students from discovering their own truths and insights. The lectures and the texts do all that sort of thing for you. They provide a way in which students can cover up their true selves by finding a vocabulary acceptable to most people and a set of facts that are generally known among people generally considered to be generally educated.

Once this skill of covering up has been acquired, students may never be called upon to say what they really think or feel at any point in their education or in later life. This is what makes bores and produces college graduates who are ignorant and dull but successful and plausible. For a teacher who cares about teaching, there is nothing as exciting as students who are ignorant, who come to you uncorrupted by other people's knowledge of the things you know most about. I think it is wrong to judge students, especially when they are freshmen, by how much they know, since if they knew everything they should know, they would not need to be in college.

We need, then, a new philosophy for a new time; we need a redirection of our educational energies to create fresh ideas for the redirection of American society. I recommend for our consideration a definition of the elements in a new philosophy expressed by Martha Graham: "There is a vitality, a life-force, an energy, a quickening which is translated through you into action, and because there is only one of you in all time, this expression is unique. And if you block it, it will never exist through any other medium and be lost. The world will not have it."

What Graham has said, not only in this illuminating passage but through her total attitude to life and through the expression of her art, defines an idea that must infuse any philosophy of education designed to release the talents of individuals. The forms of dance that Graham created are free forms—that is to say, they are forms newly created to express new truth that she found impossible to express in any of the ways that dancers, choreographers, and playwrights had taken before her. Hers was not a rejection of the past nor was it a refusal to accept her own tradition. The ancient dance forms of the East, the content of Puritan history, and the classic mythology of Greece are all components of her art, an art that has transformed the past and transcended the limitations of a time and place far different from our own. The intellectual content of this art derives from sources as modern as Freud and as old as Sophocles. But there is an energy and a particular quality in American life that Graham felt, that she made part of herself in her art, and that she translated into action. This is the same force that Whitman recognized and that he, too, created new forms to express.

But the way to find that form and that energy that is truly our own—a form that is not European, not Russian, not anything but itself—is to learn how to be sincere and honest in feelings and judgment, how to be bold and courageous enough freely to proclaim a devotion or a belief, to recognize something that perhaps no one else will either like or approve; but nevertheless to recognize it, work with it, try it out, fearing neither success nor failure, courting no approval and posing no martyrdom, but doing everything in one's power to look at it freshly and honestly. This is the way to personal independence and personal freedom. It is also the way to a national goal that can transcend the confused and timid philosophy now infecting American life.

Nowhere is the confusion and timidity to be seen more clearly than in our public debates about education. All of us have had direct experience with one or another of the problems we face in American education. We are the ones who know about the shortages of funds, the weaknesses in teaching, the deficiencies in quality, and the lack of social energy. We are also the ones who know about the enormous resources of talent and idealism in American youth, their lively minds, and their willing hearts. We have seen at first hand the dedication of teachers who care; we have seen the rich possibilities of intellectual and social advance in every aspect of American culture. We have seen some of those advances take place.

As a justification for remodeling our educational system, it is said that we need to spend more time, money, and energy on the "hard, scientific subjects and less on the time-wasting efforts of those in the arts and social studies who have blindly followed John Dewey in his concern for the individual child and for human values." Let us accept the challenge in exactly the terms in which it is made. It is true that there are weaknesses in our educational system. In the effort to provide a democratic education for all children according to their talents and needs, we have stretched our resources past the limit. There simply aren't enough good teachers to do what we are trying to do. In trying to match the growth of our population with an equivalent growth in our educational system, we have placed a burden on the existing system that it has not been able to carry. We have not spent enough money, although we have it at hand. We have spent it on other things—on motor cars, entertainment, luxuries, roads, and ten or twelve kinds of rockets that won't go off. If we had the money now spent on just one of those rockets, we could build a new school system almost anywhere.

It is also true that we have not asked as much of our students as they are willing and able to do. We have wasted time and energy in developing massive athletic programs, trivial extracurricular activities, and a fun-and-games approach to a great many subjects. But is the cure for this to keep these main defects and to add more blocks of science and mathematics while we allow the arts and the humanities to languish? Do we not need just as many educated men and women in the fields of public affairs, public health, poetry, social work, politics, theater, education, dance, medicine, public administration, painting, and government? Do we not need scientists and engineers who combine with knowledge and skill of a practical kind a sensitivity to human values, a sense of social responsibility, and an understanding and an appreciation of the arts? The widest sweep of imagination, the deepest level of intuition, the great command of insight are as necessary to the true scientist as they are to the poet or to the philosopher.

"Both science and art," says W. H. Auden,

> are spiritual activities, not practical, whatever practical applications may be derived from their results. Disorder, lack of meaning, are spiritual, not physical, discomforts; order and sense are spiritual and not physical satisfactions. The subject and the methods of the scientist and the artist differ, but their impulse is the same, the impulse which is at work in anyone who, having taken the same walk several times, finds that the distance seems shorter; what has happened is that, consciously or unconsciously, he has divided the walk into stages, thus making a memorable structure out of what at first was a structureless flux of novelty.

It is with this conception of science and its relation to our culture and to art that we educators must be concerned. The growth of science is the one ultimate, unavoidable fact that revolutionized the organization of knowledge and of society during the last century. No country that fails to develop a system of education in which science is a major force and from which imaginative and devoted scientists emerge can hope to deal with the problems of a modern, industrialized, international society. But the way to achieve scientific and cultural strength and, therefore, to contribute to international leadership is not to convert our educational institutions to the production of science students. It is to raise the level of quality in all forms of education and to provide both scientist and nonscientist alike with the rich experience that only the enjoyment of the arts and sciences can bring. The scientific spirit is not opposed to the aesthetic, the moral, or the social. It is a spirit of enlightenment, of social advance, and of creative thought. Let us not do it the dishonor of isolating it as a technique or trying to overcome it with flattery.

I wish to return to the topic with which I began—the definition of the intellect and its relation to art. There is a great deal of loose thinking about this. There are a great many inscrutable statements made by painters and sculptors, among others, about what they are doing. When narrowed down to something that can be recognized by the intellect, they say either "I don't know what I'm doing" or "I am doing something so private that I cannot tell you what it is." The unconscious has a new status and is often confused with creative imagination. I would like to say one or two things about the unconscious and about the stream of consciousness in the work of the artist. I ask, "The stream of whose consciousness?" Some people's unconscious is a great, dull area with some obvious things in it, which we all have, but not everyone's unconscious is equally interesting. The mere exposure of the unconscious does no honor to art.

I wish to speak, too, of the attitude that prevails among modern educators who are enlightened, who accept the arts, and who, in some ways, have accepted the unconscious as the main source of human value. This has had an effect on a range of activities, all the way from child rearing to the criticism of art. There is a psychological as well as social sophistication in young people who have been brought up with enlightenment, who understand the arts, who have received the psychological understanding of parents, teachers, and everyone else. This combines to produce a political conservatism and an acceptance of social reality and the kindnesses of other people just as they stand, without a wish to change society in any way but only to criticize it and to criticize such things as "them," mass culture, and mass education. You will recognize this type of rebel, a member of the "shoe" (as it is called) subculture in J. D. Salinger's writing; for example, when his character Zooey speaks of how his older brothers, Seymour and Buddy, told him and his sister at a very early age "what it's all about," which amounts to how false everything is: "These two bastards got us nice and early and made us into freaks with freakish standards, that's all. We're the Tattooed Lady, and we're never going to have a minute's peace, the rest of our lives, till everybody else is tattooed, too. . . . The minute I'm in a room with somebody who has the usual number of ears, I turn into a goddam *seer* or a human hatpin."

The dilemma for sophisticated students is that often they are too intelligent to accept the values of their society, yet they need desperately to belong to a community to which they can be loyal. They therefore rebel against the authority, and at the same time they are not quite sure they want to go on being a human hatpin. They have been taught to be critical of established values, but they have become tired of being themselves all the time.

This brings me to the role of the unconscious in directing the thinking of enlightened educators. We have developed a progressive movement in which a whole array of modern devices in education that have been considered valuable and advanced have been put into action. We have developed in the progressive environment students who are unable to rebel productively because there is nothing to rebel against. They are asked all the time to be themselves. A great deal of the time the self they are asked to be is so unformed that they don't know what it is or how to be it. But this doesn't stop them from trying, and they develop a tremendous interest in themselves and a tremendous interest in all those who are interested in them. On one hand, they ask for guidance and authority and intellectual discipline; on the other, they won't accept anything that anyone tells them on the grounds that that is just the way of authority and that is just discipline. They believe in the right of personal decision, free choice, and free speech but only for other students, not for teachers or parents. As one student at a progressive college put it: "We would rather defend someone's right to say something than to listen to what's being said."

The progressive, advanced, enlightened, modern students, who love modern art, have a problem in that from birth—or perhaps even in the preconception period—they have been treated with enlightenment and understanding. This has meant that the older line of authority that used to guide the children has been removed, and in a world in which they are not ordered around but told to choose their way, they may stifle in an atmosphere of kindly, overall approval. The intellectual discipline that they are in search of is unavailable. In an atmosphere of this kind, too thin in the oxygen of strong parental emotion, the young often feel a deep emotional fatigue from continually being forced to make their own decisions before they have had enough experience to be able to do so.

With all this going on, it is natural for modern, aesthetically sophisticated children to become clinical about themselves and about others, including their parents. I have heard children of seventeen and eighteen discuss with their parents the proper way their parents should be handling them. Such children are often inclined to invent psychological difficulties and their solutions in order to satisfy a need for self-expression, and the possession of the right kind of psychological difficulties can attract its own social prestige.

The model for this type of young person is different from that of the regular high school student who has not been touched by the enlightenment of modern attitudes nor has been exposed to as many books and ideas that are considered "cool." But it is similar in its attitude of in-groupness and clannishness. It shows itself sometimes in a special form of intellectual and aesthetic snobbery about modern art, a snobbery of not being snobbish or of feeling morally and aesthetically superior and more intensely equal than anyone else.

I think it is fair to raise the question of the strength and vitality of our culture now that we have sources of enlightenment in modern psychology, in modern educational attitudes, and in modern art. I think it is fair to ask what the teachers of art and the teachers of the arts in general are doing about it. Sometimes, I feel that many teachers are doing very little about it, except to encourage people to paint and sculpt in any way they wish. If a plain citizen questions the principle that the impulse of the subconscious is the ultimate determinant of true art, he or she is often quietly ignored in the way one does the partially deranged.

We need to face the fact that a great deal of romantic nonsense is being talked about what the practice of the creative arts does and can do for humanity and the country at large. We need to be clear about the way in which the discipline of the visual arts can become a means of learning how to think, how to see, and how to understand, at a higher level of understanding, many things other than art—science, for example. We also need to remember that once the student has become involved in the practice of an art, there are many ways in which the culture in which the art exists can be understood and must be understood, and that the student must learn to profit from knowing in some detail the history, economics, politics, and philosophy of a civilization that supports cultural values and a concern for the arts. Again, the gap between science and art is unfortunate. The gap between art and a knowledge of social, political, and economic circumstances is equally unfortunate.

I am struck with the fact that those who have the most opportunity to know these things and to do something about them are quite often those who feel that the responsibility to act belongs to someone else, usually an administrator. We are all responsible, both for our own students and for our country. I do not propose that we mount an effort to defeat rival nations with superior works of art or a more intense concern with aesthetic values. I do propose that we work where we are to persuade our students to engage themselves in the enterprise of learning, through the arts, to develop a sensibility and a means of judging good from bad, true from false, and beautiful from ugly.

When we have a culture in which our students, their parents, and our school and college graduates hold to standards of sensibility, then we will have a culture of which we can be proud and that, in terms of world opinion, can command its own respect. Our government does not yet realize that our cultural policy must be one, if it is to be effective, that makes no boast of its cultural virtues, that makes no boast that this system of political democracy produces better art than any other, but that just quietly allows the works to speak for themselves.

Why then, in a country so interested in human values, so concerned for education, so full of idealism and opportunity for every kind of cultural advantage, should there be a confusion of aims and a lack of intellectual purpose? Why, as a friend of mine asked recently, should students sometimes starve in the midst of plenty? To which my friend answered, quoting the famous Zen Buddhist story: "It is too clear, and so it is hard to see. A man once searched for a fire with lighted lantern. Had he known what fire was, he could have cooked his rice much sooner."

This is your opportunity. You know what fire is.

Part Two
How We Do It

If every child in every school from his entrance until his graduation from high school or college were given the opportunity to experience dance as a creative art, and if his dancing kept pace with his developing physical, mental, and spiritual needs, the enrichment of his adult life might reach beyond any results we can now contemplate.

It is only in art that all the aspects of man's complex nature are united in expression.

—MARGARET H'DOUBLER,
Dance: A Creative Art Experience

6
A Teacher Remembers (New Beginning in America)

ANNELISE MERTZ

It was curiosity and my love for dance that brought me to America, the cradle of modern dance. I had performed as a dancer all over Europe with renowned companies such as the State Opera of Berlin and the municipal theaters of Dusseldorf and Darmstadt, toured with the Kurt Jooss Dance Theater, and soloed with my own dances. By the time I had accomplished all this, I was more than ready to explore the dance scene in America. I wanted to see for myself how America had developed while the arts in Europe were almost destroyed during a most devastating war.

I took the first opportunity offered me and landed in Chicago in the mid-1950s, not knowing anyone there in my profession. Talking to people, I quickly discovered that a few had heard about Martha Graham but that they hardly knew the American art form called modern dance or the great artists associated with it. This was quite a blow to my great expectations. The majority of people thought I was speaking about ballroom dance.

After an intensive search, I found a small organization concerned with dance. With its help, I began teaching master classes. Shortly afterward, the University of Illinois asked me to replace its only dance teacher for one semester. At that time, they had a branch at Navy Pier in Chicago. I gladly accepted, not knowing what to expect. Classes were held on the large stage of a huge auditorium that extended way out into the lake at the end of the pier. I felt like I was teaching in the middle of the lake, and this gave me a wonderful sense of freedom—unfortunately, not for long. I was shocked by the setup of my first class, which had approximately forty to fifty students. Dance was part of the physical education department, and I had to share the auditorium with volleyball players. The department unrealistically thought that putting up small screens on the large stage where I was teaching would eliminate the volleyball noises.

I can hardly remember any details of how I was able to teach six hours every day under such circumstances while still struggling with the English language.

The students were lethargic and unable to concentrate (a small wonder, under those conditions). One student remarked in her evaluation, "She is too good for us; we are not interested." Two students saved my sanity. One, a girl from Israel, was very mature, with a good background in dance. The other was a male psychology student. The student newspaper proclaimed, "The first male student ever to sign up for a dance class at this university! Is he a man?" This was fall 1956. My entire semester was a nightmare. I was relieved when it was finished but greatly surprised when I heard of a petition signed by over one hundred students wanting me to stay.

Shortly after that, I received an invitation from Washington University in St. Louis, where they had heard about my teaching in Chicago. To my astonishment, they offered me a full-time position without a personal interview. They showed no interest in my professional background as a dancer, wanting only to know of my degrees—a bit puzzling for me as a newcomer to this country.

When I arrived in St. Louis in January 1957, I found a small but pleasant dance studio with a bouncy floor, a nice change after my experience in Chicago. This time I found myself in the women's physical education department. Unfortunately, the studio was partitioned from the swimming pool, separated from it by only a thin wall that was, again, not soundproofed. A smaller sidewall extended only halfway to the ceiling. On the other side were several hair dryers. When the dryers were in use, their noise forced people to converse loudly, which was not very helpful to me trying to teach on the other side. Finally after several years, the wall with the hair dryers was closed, and I came to an agreement with the department that no synchronized swimming would be scheduled during my dance classes. However, in my sixteen years of teaching in the studio, the wall to the pool was never soundproofed. The students and I had no choice but to put up with the usual noise of an indoor swimming pool and the annoying smell of chlorine.

Up to this point, my teaching experience in America had given me the impression that dance at universities was looked upon only as a glorified exercise class for women—and I was expected to teach it that way. This created a problem for me, because I wanted to teach dance as a creative contemporary art form.

Through advanced research in the last century, science has given us a much fuller understanding of the complete relationship of body and mind. This knowledge, combined with lessening religious intolerance and a changed social attitude (mainly after World War I), resulted in the development of a different form of dance—modern dance. The seeds came from America through the forerunners of modern dance: Isadora Duncan, Ruth St. Denis, and Ted Shawn. The actual pioneers of modern dance were Martha Graham, Doris Humphrey, and Charles Weidman, because they were the first to develop a new theory and technique. I'd like to add Hanya Holm to this list, because she brought the Mary Wigman technique and theory of German modern dance to this country. Margaret H'Doubler, founder of the country's first dance program in 1926 at the University of Wisconsin, stated in her book *Dance: A Creative Art Experience*, "Modern Dance is a concept—a point of view—and not a prescribed system. It is dance as it is conceived today in terms of its science, philosophy and art." Louis Horst, who was a composer and accompanist for Graham, wrote with Carroll Russell in the book *Modern Dance Forms in Relation to Other Modern Arts* about a more extensive and quite poetic approach: "The pioneers in modern dance and their successors recaptured the relation that the primitive has to his body—an intimacy with the muscle tensions of daily movements which had been lost to modern men. This is not at all the ballet dancer's awareness of line, of speed or balance, and dramatic portrayal of a role. It is, rather, an inner sensitivity to every one of the body's parts, to the power of its whole, and to the space in which it carves designs. The great quest was to find ways to attain this sensitivity, and manners in which to discipline it for communication."

Modern dance is the form I chose to teach because I believe that, in its analytical and creative approach to movement, it can stimulate the imagination and the intellect. It strives for the development of the body in an integrated way and serves as a valuable source of self-awareness. If it is taught with these goals in mind, it can contribute greatly to a humanistic education, which I think is an antidote to our increasingly mechanized life. Another goal for me was to cultivate my students' aesthetic awareness and refinement of motion. The big problem was how much I could accomplish in just three and a half months, because many students took dance only for one semester, and each class met only two or three times weekly for an hour and a half.

At that time, one physical education course was required for graduation, and students could choose between volleyball, swimming, dance, and so on. I discovered that the expectation of most students taking dance was to get exercise and to lose weight. Their previous experience with live performances was mainly at musicals performed in their high schools. At their age, I had already seen many great professional performances in dance, drama, and opera in Europe. For the first time, I understood what an important education I had received through seeing these performances—one that I had taken for granted.

It was clear to me that first I had to motivate the students before I could teach them. I did this partly through reading assignments, discussions, and of course, through movement that included improvisation and basic technique. I tried to make them aware of the body as an instrument of expression in daily life and in dance and drama as well. Through simple exercises, they began to understand how the body should work as a unified entity and how emotional impressions have their effect on movement and vice versa. Experimenting with movement means exploring shape, space, energy, time, and motion—these are the media for composing in dance just as sound and time are the media for composing in music. Painting is concerned with space and color. In fact, in its composition, dance is the only art form that is equally concerned with time and space. Working consciously with principles of movement helps students to develop greater kinesthetic awareness, which is closely connected with the feeling of identity. Technique and theory classes should emphasize investigating movement in these terms, as opposed to just practice drills and routines. This kind of involvement is extremely valuable in the process of learning and maturing. I am not a believer in "appreciation" courses, in which students sit down and hear about the arts without ever getting involved in a creative process themselves.

To my great delight, most of the students responded well to my teaching approach. As one student stated: "Along with a more unified purpose of motion, this awareness of your body leads you to become aware of all other things; nature becomes much more vivid in your eyes. It is really an awareness of everything around you. You widen your scope of concern from the errands you're running and everything around you more or less wakes up and you become aware of the world along with yourself." Another student wrote: "It may seem trivial, but the biggest thing for me in this class was becoming aware that there really is an art to movement."

But there were also students who were completely caught in the web of the educational system. One, for example, wrote: "One criticism I have is that it is too time-demanding outside of class. The time I needed for making a 'study' could have been used for studying for an exam, which is more important because of the units of credits received for the semester." Students who are so credit-oriented are not easy to teach.

Gradually, I developed a group consisting of ten or twelve very dedicated and talented students, and I toyed with the idea of giving lecture demonstrations. I wanted to develop more understanding of modern dance on the campus as well as in the greater St. Louis community. In my classes at that time, I had to cover everything in one course—technique, theory, and just a bit of history and composition—to give the students a more complete picture of dance as an art form. For the very brief compositional studies (one or two minutes long), I gave them simple problems, for example: "inner and outer focus," "breath rhythm, metric rhythm," "sculptural, motional" design, or establishing a relationship between two parts of the body. One might compare such studies with simple etudes in music. I prepared the lecture for the demonstration and put these creative studies together in such a way that they began to relate to and complement each other when performed. We presented the lecture demonstration wherever we could find a large enough space with a fairly decent floor—gymnasiums, cafeterias, and so on. We were all very excited and nervous at the same time. It was the first performing experience for the students and my first time speaking English in front of an audience. I don't know who learned more, the students or me. As it turned out, we both were successful and continued to have good response at subsequent lecture demonstrations. I was gratified to sense that audience interest in dance was growing.

In March 1957, an event occurred that had a great impact on my life as a teacher and a choreographer. There was to be a concert of contemporary music by the composer Harry Partch. It took place in a dreary high school auditorium in south St. Louis. A few minutes into the concert, to my great surprise, dancers came out onstage. No dance had been announced. Their performance and the choreography was highly imaginative and original and so exciting that the dance stole the show. I was surprised and fascinated at the same time. After the performance, I talked immediately to the artistic director. I discovered that he was one of the great choreographers of American modern dance—Alwin Nikolais. He invited me to come to Connecticut College for the summer of 1957. It was there that I met many of the great figures of American modern dance who were working in the east at that time. I studied with several of them: Nikolais, Martha Graham, Doris Humphrey, Jose Limon, and Murray Louis. I also studied with a German dancer of the Wigman school, Margaret Dietz. The experience was invaluable. My study with Nikolais was the most challenging and creative one I ever had, and we became lifelong friends. He became my mentor! Besides being an outstanding choreographer, Nikolais was also a musician, a painter, a composer, and a designer—a real Renaissance artist. After two years in the United States, my expectations that there was an important and exciting art movement in this country called modern dance were finally confirmed. Unfortunately, too few people knew about it. After six weeks at Connecticut College, I returned to St. Louis refreshed, stimulated, and full of plans for the future, determined to make this art form more familiar to the public.

At Connecticut College, I met many gifted professional dancers and talked to them not only about giving performances at Washington University but also about my problem of not having any budget. They agreed to accept any fee we could afford, based on the sale of tickets. Raising money was a totally foreign idea for me, because the arts in Europe are mainly supported by the government so that artists can fully concentrate on their work. My first choice was Daniel Nagrin. Students were in awe. They had never seen such a strong and dynamic man dancing. Another artist appearing later was Katherine Litz. Both concerts were a great success. When the Jose Limon Company approached me because they would be performing near St. Louis, I quickly agreed. The company of six or eight came in their own minibus, and I lodged them with friends because I had no money for a hotel. I did the same with the Merce Cunningham Company. For those performances, I had to find a high school auditorium near Washington University. I can still see John Cage preparing a piano for the performance by putting nails into the strings, to my great horror. I required my students to attend all performances. The students resisted a bit at first, but when I explained that watching a dance performance is equal to reading a book for a course, they began to understand. Though somewhat bewildered (especially with Cunningham), they liked it, and we had several lively discussions.

My dance classes had grown so much by the early 1960s that I was given permission to hire another instructor. I purposely chose a man, Myron Nadel. He came with his wife, Constance, who was also a dancer. This was, of course, very convenient. Both had graduated from the Julliard School in New York. I also started a Saturday morning program in creative dance for children, because to my knowledge, nothing like that existed in the entire city. In connection with this program, I developed a certification program for teaching dance in the public schools. Up to that time, certified physical education teachers were automatically allowed to teach dance, despite having little or no knowledge of it.

Finally, after five years of hard work, I was provided by the Washington University Student Union with a small budget for a dance performance on campus, in a facility with a rather poor stage for dance. It was the best they had at that time. The abstract poems by Edith Sitwell and the music by William Walton were so close to my heart that I wanted to add some choreography to make it a visual experience. The piece was called *Façade*. The stage got a creative boost by two huge collages of *Falling Man* by Ernest Trova as the background. They are now at the Museum of Modern Art in New York. The collages were a bit overwhelming on the small stage but added greatly to the atmosphere of the performance. The poems were recited by one drama faculty member, the late Herb Metz, and a graduate student, Charlotte Moore, who is today the artistic director of the Irish Repertory Theater in New York. A small orchestra was supplied by the music department. The dance faculty, including myself, Myron Nadel, his wife, and a male instructor from another university, Willis Ward, performed with the students, who were all female. I had created the choreography as well as the costumes, which for budget reasons had to be simple. It was far from a flawless performance. The microphone gave out halfway through, and some of the sparse lighting burned out. But what a surprise that, after all, the audience loved it. One professor remarked: "With this show, the performing arts at Washington University came of age." The critic for the *St. Louis Post-Dispatch* wrote: "It must be noted that the intrusion of Modern Dance into the urbane, highly ordered world of Sitwell and Walton was diverting." The students danced with great spirit and enthusiasm. With this performance, I founded the Washington University Dance Theater.

Being more settled and accepted now, I began to push much harder to have dance removed from the physical education department. My idea was to persuade the drama faculty to leave the mighty umbrella of the English department and unite with dance. A committee was formed, and for one year we had meetings with some very stormy discussions. The English department was very accommodating, and so was the women's physical education division, but the athletic director, whom I had hardly met, suddenly discovered his love for dance and did not want to see it leave his department. Finally, he was persuaded to give it a try, and the difficult step was accomplished. In the fall of 1966, the performing arts department was created. I purposely suggested that name, fearing that if we had called it a theater department, that would have been taken to mean only drama. For me, who grew up in Europe, dance, drama, and opera are all forms of theater.

In 1966, the National Endowment for the Arts was created in this country and was of great assistance to the lives of starving dancers. With the financial help of the NEA, dance companies could develop programs and tour with them. They also began to ask for contracts with a set fee. Still not having any budget from the university, I felt it was impossible for me to meet this new demand. The idea of organizing a nonprofit organization independent of the university came to my mind. As a result, with the help of friends (mostly painters), the Dance Concert Society, later renamed Dance St. Louis, was formed. All board members worked hard as volunteers, and my living room was the office. It was the modest beginning of what is now one of the most well-known presenters of dance in this country. We started with an emphasis on modern dance because this American art form was hardly known to the public in St. Louis. Our first performance was by the Murray Louis Dance Company from New York. It was the right choice for a strong beginning. We had to search again for an auditorium and found a nice little theater in a private high school. The lighting equipment was, of course, not quite sufficient for this professional company from New York. Nevertheless, we got a wonderful response. Encouraged by our successful start, we became quite adventurous and in 1968 brought the Nikolais Dance Theatre (also from New York) to the Kiel Opera House (a theater of three thousand seats). I was president at this time, and I still have nightmares when I remember how, without any experience in management and with hardly any volunteers, I managed to fill this big house with about eighteen hundred people.

Many more important steps were accomplished in those early years, but finally we could see the light—in the fall of 1973, the Edison Theater was inaugurated on campus. Finally, dance and drama had a decent place in which to work and perform. A new chapter in our professional life had begun. Dance had now moved into a newly established performing arts department with a modest program for a dance major, which I had developed while I was still in the physical education department. My immediate plans were therefore to extend this program by offering different-level courses in technique and theory as well as in composition, improvisation, ballet, dance history, repertory, and kinesiology. But this ambition required more faculty. It took a lot of persuasion and sometimes serious confrontation to get them. Of course, one always had to prove the demand through sufficient enrollment. This was not always easy since most dance and drama classes have to be kept small to be effective. Over the years, I was able to hire two full-time instructors, two part-time instructors, and a full-time musician. In 1974, after the new theater was opened on campus, I founded the Summer Dance Institute. Again, it was a modest beginning with just one guest artist, Phyllis Lamhut from New York, added to our faculty. She taught most of the courses for four weeks with an improvised performance at the end of the term. At a later date, when I was able to connect the Summer Dance Institute with the Mississippi River Festival, I was able to engage a whole company. The dancers were teaching at Washington University during the week and performing on weekends at the festival. The festival, which mainly offered a series of classical music concerts, was held in a large tent on the campus of Southern Illinois University in Edwardsville. It was a successful experience for a few years until the money was cut off. Then all was quiet again on both campuses.

In spite of many frustrations, we now had a brand-new dance studio and an excellent modern stage on which to perform. The Washington University Dance Theater gave one full theatrical performance every year, usually in March or April. This gave us enough time for extensive rehearsals, because the students were not always available (vacation, finals, etc.), and it was also fair to the dance faculty who had to rehearse in the evening and on weekends as well as carry a full teaching load. The choreography for the performance was done by individual faculty members, and most of them performed with the students. In this way, we were able to bring the performance to a professional level, and the students felt honored and gave their best. We also felt this was the best learning experience for students. What I wanted to avoid was a student talent show for Mom and Pop where you throw as many students as possible onstage, many of them uncertain as to why they are there or what they are doing. I always made students aware that the stage is a special place, and that they have to earn the right to perform on it. In addition to the annual performance, students of the composition classes gave an informal but theatrical presentation in the dance studio each semester before an invited audience. A theatrical setting was provided by students from stage lighting classes and by others from costume design classes. I was amazed at the wonderful inventiveness of the students, who were very often unaware of their own previously untapped creative talents. Through all those performances, we slowly developed a very loyal audience that grew every year.

In the first years of the new theater, we faced some problems in the staging of a dance performance. A full-time technical director had to be hired. Most of the applicants had graduated from universities, and their knowledge was almost entirely in drama; they had very little or no experience in stage lighting for dance. For our performances, I had to engage special lighting designers from New York, who could also give lectures on the subject. Lighting is to dance what scenery is to a play. We also had similar difficulties with costume designers. Dance costumes are seldom period costumes but mostly free, abstract designs supporting the idea of the dance. A designer working for dance has to understand how the body moves and how a certain fabric and lighting can enhance the movements.

I was often asked why the Washington University Dance Theater gives only one performance on the main stage, while two plays are staged by the drama faculty. There are several reasons for this. Generally, a play is already written, and after an extensive reading, the director can begin with the rehearsals. The situation for dance is very different. The dance has to be choreographed first (equivalent to the writing of the play) before it can be directed. This is a time-consuming process. Usually choreographing and directing work together if the choreographer is also the director, but they are two different disciplines.

Presently, several notations for dance exist, but it would be easier for choreographers if they had only one notation as in music. The best and most accurate one we have is probably Labanotation, but it is so difficult it has to be practiced continuously—in other words, you have to become a notator. If you are a teacher, choreographer, and maybe a dancer as well, it is often impossible to find the time and energy to add the profession of notator to your life. To my knowledge, there is not a great deal of notated choreography available, and not many dancers have become notators. Notated choreography works best in conjunction with a videotape. This is very costly and is hardly in line with a typical dance performance budget. I studied Labanotation for three years in Europe, but today I can hardly read one small movement phrase. I have preserved some of my choreography through videotapes only. That means that only I, as the choreographer, or perhaps a dancer who performed the dance, might be able to reconstruct it accurately. A video is not accurate enough, because it is two-dimensional, while dance is three-dimensional. These reasons alone—and I have not stated them all—explain why choreographers have very little material to fall back on but have to develop new, original choreography most of the time. It takes time to create new choreography, and dance also needs a special space to perform. These are some of the reasons that dance has a smaller audience in comparison to music or drama.

Of the many dance events we staged at the Edison Theater, I would like to mention two particularly special ones. The first was a ragtime festival that we repeated once. Steven Radek, our musical director and a well-known ragtime pianist, invited many of the renowned players, including Eubie Blake and Max Morath. They all were greatly surprised when they saw dances choreographed to "Maple Leaf Rag," "Cascades," "Charleston Rag," and so on. Some of the dances reflected the atmosphere of the 1920s but were choreographed in the modern dance idiom. They were created by Gale Ormiston (artist-in-residence) and myself and were performed by faculty and students. These performances of live music and dance received an enthusiastic response from the large audience. In 1979, we brought one of the programs to Ireland, where it enjoyed the same success.

The other event was *Façade*. After twenty years, I wanted to restage it again in 1983. It turned out that I had no recording of the 1963 performance and could not remember any of the original choreography (which indicates how ephemeral dance is). However, it would have been necessary to create new choreography anyway, because this time we had a modern theater with a large stage, offering us more technical possibilities. We also had more better-trained dancers and better musicians conducted by English guest artist Nikolas McGegan, who worked wonders with them. We also had a good costume designer, Bonnie Kruger, and I invited the lighting designer Ruth Grauert from New York. How wonderful to work in such an environment! Gale Ormiston and I each choreographed half of the nineteen dances. There were twenty-one poems in *Façade,* but the dances were not interpretations of the poems—instead, they added an additional voice and visual design to the atmosphere of the forty-five-minute piece.

Shortly before my retirement, I was able to take to Berlin, Germany, one special performance with two faculty members, Gale Ormiston and Michael Ballard, one guest artist, Janice Brenner (all three former members of the Nikolais and Murray Louis companies), and one graduate student, Scott Loebl. They were part of my professional company called St. Louis Dancers. It was very gratifying and exciting for me to bring some of my work from America to my hometown after so many years. We performed at the Academy of the Arts, which had a beautiful theater, and we had approximately twenty curtain calls at the end of each performance. The critic for the Berlin paper *Tagesspiegel* (Daily Mirror) wrote: "The Americanized choreographer Annelise Mertz from Berlin does the finale with aplomb, with the choreography 'Ceremonial Rites' (music by Philip Glass). Three dancing men grasp giant stiffened red coats that provide perplexing optical mysteries. Are these robes of priests or wings of ghosts?"

Since its opening, Washington University's Edison Theater has scheduled many excellent professional companies of modern dance, which has been an important art education for the students. Our students were required to attend these performances, which we discussed in class afterwards. Most had been familiar only with musicals, pop concerts, and sports events. Through our work at Washington University, including the Edison Theater, and through the efforts of Dance St. Louis in presenting professional dance companies from all over the world, we helped develop the awareness, interest, and knowledge of dance as an art not only on campus but in the city of St. Louis as well. Being retired now and looking back at those thirty-three years (from 1957 to 1990) with all the ups and downs, I have asked myself very often, "Was it worth it?" Each time, I have to answer it with a wholehearted "yes." I felt that teaching had a stimulating effect on my performing and choreographing, and vice versa. Furthermore, helping young people mature, guiding them to get a sense of direction for finding their right place in life, was always rewarding for me. College is the time when most students seriously begin this searching process. By fostering their creative talents, I believe, all the arts can make a valuable contribution to their growing up. I think that dance, if taught as a creative art, is especially suited for young people, because it engages the whole human being—emotionally, mentally, and physically.

Michael Ballard *(right)*, a
former assistant professor
of dance at Washington
University, and Scott
Loebl, a former dance
major at Washington
University, in *Calligraph
for Martyrs,* choreo-
graphed by Murray Louis,
artistic director of the
Murray Louis Dance
Company. Photograph
by Brian Gordon; printed
with permission from
Scott Loebl.

Michael Ballard and
Scott Loebl in *Calligraph
for Martyrs.* Photograph
by Brian Gordon; printed
with permission from
Scott Loebl.

Amy Schactman, a former dance major at Washington University, in her own solo dance. Photograph by David Henschel, Washington University Photographic Service; printed with permission from Amy Schactman.

Ruth Füglistaller, a former dance major at Washington University, performing her own compositional study. Photograph by Herb Weitman, Washington University Photographic Service.

Washington University dance student performing her own compositional study titled "Shape." Photograph by Tom Stewart, Washington University Photographic Service.

Annelise Mertz, a professor emerita and former director of the dance division at Washington University, teaching a class in modern dance. Photograph by David Henschel, Washington University Photographic Service.

Annelise Mertz and Murray Louis conversing in the dance studio. Photograph by Washington University Photographic Service.

Gale Ormiston, a former senior artist in residence at Washington University, performing "The Navy Blue Ghost" from the suite *Façade;* choreography and structural design by Ormiston, with lighting design by Ruth Grauert. Photograph by Washington University Photographic Service; printed with permission from Gale Ormiston.

Scott Loebl, Michael Ballard, and Gale Ormiston in "Ceremonial Rites (The Men),"
choreographed by Annelise Mertz. Photograph by Robert L. Stevens, Washington University Photographic Service; printed with permission from Scott Loebl and Gale Ormiston.

Michael Ballard in
"Ceremonial Rites (The
Men)," choreographed
by Annelise Mertz.
Photograph by Wash-
ington University
Photographic Service.

"Ceremonial Rites (The Women)," choreographed by Annelise Mertz. Photograph by Washington University Photographic Service.

Sara Shelton, a former artist in residence at Washington University, in "The Wonderful Widow of 18 Springs," choreographed by Annelise Mertz. Photograph by Bibi Stromberg; printed with permission from Sara Shelton Mann and Bonnie Jacobson.

Sara Shelton in "The Wonderful Widow of 18 Springs." Photograph by Washington University Photographic Service; printed with permission from Sara Shelton Mann.

Jumay Chu, a guest artist at Washington University, in "Youkali," choreographed by Annelise Mertz. Photograph by Washington University Photographic Service; printed with permission from Jumay Chu.

"Under the Roof," one of the themes explored in an improvisational workshop in creative movement and dance for children conducted by Annelise Mertz at the Space Place, a structure inside the St. Louis Art Museum. Photograph by Washington University Photographic Service.

"Above the Roof," another theme explored at the Space Place. Photograph by Washington University Photographic Service.

"Building Spaces," another theme explored at the Space Place. Photograph by Washington University Photographic Service.

7
A Male Dancer's Journey

G. HOFFMAN SOTO

I grew up in a family that put a lot of importance on the physical manifestation of the spirit. Both of my grandfathers and my father were baseball players. My older brother was good at any sport he tried, and I followed in the line and had success as a high school and college basketball player. At twenty-two years of age, I stopped playing sports and found my way to the world of Yoga. As I look back, I now realize that Yoga gave me a bridge to the dance world. Yoga introduced me to a noncompetitive way of being in my body, as opposed to the I-win, you-lose mentality of sports. Because the culture and mind-set of Yoga are so different from the mind-set of athletics, studying Yoga began to open me to new possibilities in the movement world. The mid-to-late 1960s was a time for me to move out of the sports mind into the Eastern mind. This had the effect of making me a little more tolerant of what I was soon exposed to in the dance world.

THE BEGINNING

In 1969, I returned to the United States from an extended stay in Brazil and other parts of South America. I got a summer job working at a retreat center in upstate New York. A dancer friend suggested that because I was fairly flexible (Yoga) and enjoyed physical things (sports), I might enjoy taking some dance classes. She gave me an address in New York, and I promised I would check it out in the fall when I returned to the city.

Back in the city in early October, I called the studio and got the class schedule. A beginners class in Martha Graham technique was already seven classes into a sixteen-class schedule. I told them I'd rather start immediately than wait for the next session. It was OK with them. They told me I needed to buy some leotards and tights and show up at the next class. I stepped into my first dance class in the fall of 1969.

I knew this wasn't the familiar locker room because I was the only man in the men's dressing room. It was the first time I had worn leotards and tights, and I didn't know how to put them on correctly. Did the tights go over the leotards or vice versa? As it turned out, I put the tights on first and then the leotards over them. When I stepped into the studio, the first thing that caught my eye was my image in the mirror looking back at me. I couldn't believe what I saw. My legs appeared to be about eighteen inches long, my torso stretching to the ceiling and my crotch to my knees. It was as if I were standing in the fun house looking in one of those mirrors that distort the body image. I was not enjoying the view. All I could think about was how I could sneak back into the dressing room and get the hell out of there. My first dance experience was not unfolding as I had imagined. Before the thought of escape reached the muscles to move my bones, the teacher, a man, walked into the class, clapped his hands, and started class.

I moved as far to the back of the room as possible and tried to make myself invisible. The class turned out to be more foreign than I had expected or was prepared for. The vocabulary the teacher was using might as well have been Mongolian, for all I understood. I knew the words but had no idea how to translate the words being used to describe movements into actual movements. The teacher, sensing my complete bewilderment, chose to ignore me. I don't know if it was an act of mercy or what, but he pretended that I wasn't there, which was fine with me, because I was pretending that I wasn't there, too. He never spoke to me, acknowledged me, corrected me, or helped me and never gave even a glance or a nod in my direction. I had no clue as to what, why, or how to put into action what he was asking the class to do. In all fairness, the class had already met seven times and had developed a vocabulary. Coming in one-third of the way through the session was a very bad idea. I was lost in modern dance limbo. I was unbaptized and had not the possibility to enter the leotarded gates. The only salvation was that I was playing invisible and couldn't be seen flailing about like a fish out of water, or so I imagined.

When I looked at the clock, I actually began to feel good; class was almost over. It was soon to be a bad story I could laugh about with my friends. But this was a seriously bad day I was having. The teacher clapped his hands together, and I followed the herd of women to one corner of the studio. The teacher demonstrated a movement across the floor, and to my utter dismay, the other students began moving across the floor, two at a time, repeating the movement. For the uninitiated, the etiquette in dance class is that the advanced, or best, students go first, then the next best, and so on to the end, where the worst, in this case me, goes last. So let me set the scenario. I was at the end of the line, the odd number, so I had to go alone, the only man in class, unequivocally the worst student ever to walk through the studio doors, and I had no idea what I was supposed to do.

It is important to understand the context of this situation. I had been a successful athlete since I was eight years old. My early years consisted of shooting hoops, hitting line drives, and catching passes across the middle. This is how I identified myself: physically strong, coordinated, and good at what I did. This was me. All of a sudden, I was at the end of the line in this strange, new world of long-legged and long-necked New York women dancers sashaying across the floor, embodying grace and elegance. When my turn came and I saw the immense distance I had to go to get to the opposite end of the studio, I was scared to death. As I moved into the space, I realized my feet and legs, arms and shoulders, torso and head were all acting like they had never met before. Here I was, struggling to get across the floor, and at the goal line stood a very intimidating group of women dancers in their New York state of mind, waiting impatiently and unsympathetically for me to get my uncoordinated self across and off the floor. My biggest problem was the expanse of space and time to the other side of the studio. I thought I'd never get there. I cannot recall a more embarrassing and humiliating moment in my life as an athlete, martial artist, dancer, actor, or model. Every eye in the room was fixed on me (I felt), and I was tripping and stumbling along to my utter bewilderment.

In the middle of all this body-mind chaos, an amazing moment passed before me. It was like a crack in my world opened up, and I fell into a black hole of compassion for the Walter Kennedys, Vincent Hermans, and Clifford Wingers of my youth, who caught balls with their heads and behinds, tripped over their feet at least twice a day, and suffered the humiliation of years of gym classes where they were the butt of every spastic, dork, wimp, and geek joke imaginable. For four years, every day, Monday through Friday, they suffered through the humiliation of being the last one chosen on some meaningless team as everybody moaned and griped about having to take them. Then they faced a locker room full of raging, hormone-spewing teenage boys going berserk at these poor boys' naked, puny, and underdeveloped bodies. Oh God, was I working through some Karma or what? At this moment of my own utter humiliation, I was transported to my high school locker room with all the pain and suffering Walter, Vincent, and Clifford had to go through their whole teenage life. It was Karma hell.

As all things pass, so did this class. Somehow, I got through it alive. Well, my ego had certainly died a miserable and horrific death, but the rest of me made it out the door and back on to the streets. Now, thirty years later, the most extraordinary thing for me is that I went back and finished the course, and it never got better.

ARE WE HAVING FUN YET?

A friend told me that I needed to try another style of dance, because dance could, and should, be fun. At this point, that idea was so far from my experience that I couldn't quite believe her. Out of friendship and desperation, I accepted her invitation and went to an Afro-Haitian class. What a revelation! This was the exact opposite of my experience in the Martha Graham class. The Afro-Haitian dance was challenging yet big fun, and I actually had moments when I felt I was dancing. The teacher's name was Ned Williams. I'll never forget him. He was attentive and clear, and I always felt he was working with me. Even the soreness in my thighs was comforting because it brought back body memories of early season basketball practices—physical memories of soreness that was totally overwhelming yet somehow exhilarating. Walking down the steps after class, I felt my thighs screaming and my mind luxuriating in the realization that maybe dance was something for me! It was totally inspiring. This was my first *yes* to dance. I had had to push and force myself to go to the Martha Graham technique class, where I always felt uncoordinated and embarrassed about myself and my movement. I kept telling myself there must be something that I wasn't seeing, that it was good for me, and that I just wasn't getting it. In contrast, the Afro-Haitian classes made physical sense to me, and I liked myself when I was in class. The movements felt somehow familiar, comfortable, and fun. That was the impulse that thrust me into the dance world, and it still continues to move me today.

I don't want to be negative about the Martha Graham technique; it speaks for itself. What did I know about it other than my own experience? But for me, a beginner in the dance world, Martha Graham was just not the best choice. It was just too foreign to me, there was no male support, and it was much too big a stretch for this boy to make.

TO THE WEST COAST

I left New York and moved back to San Diego, where I had grown up. I enrolled in a jazz dance class at a local community college, because that was all I could find. I also began to study Tai Chi Chuan at this time. I remember how thrilled I was when my seventy-something-year-old teacher told me in his sparse

English that I moved like a girl. I knew what he meant; he was telling me I wasn't as stiff and hard as the other men he worked with, and I was happy for that. It was another positive feedback to keep me dancing.

In the summer of 1973, I moved to San Francisco and through a mutual friend met Anna Halprin. She invited me to study at the San Francisco Dancers' Workshop. I spent the summer in classes in the city, at her Marin County Mountain Home Studio, and at the Sea Ranch on the northern California coast. What Halprin was doing in her work opened me up and stretched me beyond my wildest dreams. A very positive part of this experience was the number and quality of the men dancing in Halprin's company and workshops; strong men with strong physical presences. It was comforting to be moving with a group of hardy and hearty men. It gave me a bridge from my old identity as an athlete to my new identity as a dancer. It offered me a mirror to see who I was as a man with other men. Moving and dancing with these black, brown, yellow, and white men brought my dance experience into more wholeness. It became obvious how important it was for me to dance with men and have strong male models. Up until then, I was usually the lone male, or on a good day, one of two or three men in class. In Halprin's work, the male dancers/movers were using dance to express who they were. Being amid this dynamic allowed me to begin to feel, express, and expand who I was and how I saw myself. I was moving into an exciting arena of possibilities to express and create myself in ways not previously available to me. My feelings and emotions became players in my dance and, possibly more important, began to translate into my life. I saw for the first time that a man could be strong and male, while at the same time begin to own and work with his fear, sadness, anger, joy, and sensitivity in a creative context. It was a powerful enticement for me to dance.

In saying all of the above, I am not trying to reduce or deny the importance of my experience of dancing and moving with strong and powerful women. To go out on an edge physically and have women out there with me was new and exciting for me. I had played sports at a time when women were cheerleaders, not athletes. My relationship to my physicality was through the "male thing." Now I was dancing with men and with women. Both were important in shaping my experience of dance. If I had not had the opportunity to dance and move with men, it would have completely changed the shape of my experience of dancing with women and my overall experience of dance. Moving with men felt primal and touched me on a very deep level. I see now that this relationship to male dancers was what kept me going back to dance classes.

DEVELOPMENT

In the mid-to-late 1970s, I met two male dancers, Min Tanaka and Bira Almeida, who became role models for me. They had a tremendous impact on me and were an inspiration for me as a dancer and a teacher. They opened doors for me to see what dance was and gave me direction as to where a man could take it. They allowed me to see that my very small and limited perspective on dance was just that, small and limited. They propelled me into exploring what dance could be for me.

I first saw Min Tanaka dancing in the old San Francisco Dancers' Workshop on Divisadero Street in 1978. A large Japanese man, he was painted brown and was naked except for a wrap around his genitals. He also had a huge and commanding presence. It was the first time I saw Butoh, the Japanese modern dance also referred to as "the dance of darkness" (not to be confused with Budo, which is the way of martial arts). Tanaka electrified the room and everyone in it. His movements were painfully slow and tense. He spent a lot of time on the floor assuming positions in a wide range of human and animal shapes as well as shapes of objects that were recognizable and some that were not. It was visually very different and other-worldly for me. A couple of days later, I saw Tanaka again, this time dancing in the redwoods at Anna Halprin's Mountain Home Studio. Again I was awed. He worked on a hillside and blended into his environment so completely that he would literally disappear for short periods of time. I had not seen anything like him before. I was so fascinated by Min San and what he was doing that I began to study with him there and later in Tokyo. I am not a Butoh dancer, but I was moved enough by the man and his art that I knew it was important for me to study and spend time with him. Over the years, in the San Francisco Bay area, in Tokyo, and in Amsterdam, Munich, and Paris, I saw him perform perhaps twenty times. Each time was unique, and each time, astounding. He is an incredible performer, and I still feel touched and influenced by his work.

When I was in Brazil in the late 1960s, I got a glimpse of Capoeira, the Afro-Brazilian martial art/dance form. Years later, in 1979, I found Capoeira in the San Francisco Mission District. Capoeira brings dance, music, acrobatics, and martial arts together. I fell in love with the music, the movement, and the strong feeling of *camarado,* the connection between the Capoeiristas. My teacher, Bira Almeida, or Mestre Acordeon, was another man who moved like no man I had seen before. He was smooth, fluid, powerful, and explosive. He moved as comfortably upside down as right side up and turned those he was playing with inside out. Capoeira was embodying my dream of blending martial arts and dance.

I studied with Almeida for over fourteen years. As the years passed, I was to meet and play with many strong and fluid Capoeiristas, both male and female, in the *roda* (the "wheel," or circle where the *jogo*, or play, takes place that is formed by the people surrounding the players of Capoeira, usually other Capoeiristas waiting to get into the circle). I was fortunate to meet and study with a number of beautiful and graceful Capoeiristas both here and in Europe. In my study of this dynamic art, I was constantly working on building my vocabulary of movement possibilities and then improvising and developing myself inside the roda. The pain in my knees eventually forced me to stop. I still miss Capoeira. To this day, when I'm feeling good, I will put on the music and do the *ginga*, the basic movement of Capoeira, swaying and flowing from an *armada* (spin kick) to an *esquiva* (dodging movement to the side) and then falling into an *au* (cartwheel).

CONCLUSION

At the age of fifty-three and with twenty-nine years of studying and teaching dance, movement, and martial arts behind me, I still feel the thrill of moving and dancing with men. As a teacher of dance and movement, I also feel the satisfaction of having male students. Over the years, I have become the model that I so cherished when I began dancing. I love being pushed and challenged by a man in movement and dance. It is not competition that I feel. It is more the concept of team work. To dance together requires working with, playing with, and supporting each other. To tune in to our dance partners means to help each other uncover and explore who we are. We have to learn to become more available to ourselves as well as to those with whom we are dancing. The more we bring to the dance, the more we can become the dance.

I often think how much dance has affected my life for the better. It has opened so many doors for my personal development as a man, an artist, and a human being. I often work with children, and I have observed that at a very young age, boys get an attitude about dance: "Girls dance, and boys do sports." I have been fortunate to work with a group of kids in the classroom for the past six years, some of them for all six years and some of them for three or four years. I am beginning to see that a number of these boys are now moving into another stage. They are beginning to enjoy dancing. They enjoy the expression of themselves through movement. This makes my heart soar. I feel these past years have been a blessing for me to know that I have somehow influenced these male children to understand that yes, you can play sports, and yes, you can also dance, and that these things may even complement and support each other. I recently saw a number of these boys dancing as part of a Halloween Haunted House. They were doing a piece from Michael Jackson's *Thriller*. It was great to see them so committed, looking good, having fun, and moving and grooving. I felt rewarded for all the hours of struggle to get them to participate in the classes and to just try the movements. It almost made my first dance class worth it—no, I take that back. It made it well worth it.

8
Creative Freedom, a Personal Treasure: A Tribute to Alwin Nikolais

DOROTHY M. VISLOCKY

Many years ago, while working as a counselor at a young people's camp in Maine, I had a casual crossing of paths with a dancer named Phyllis Lamhut that led me to a life-altering set of circumstances. This gift of chance, providential (divine) guidance, or sheer coincidence directed me to Henry Street Playhouse in New York, Alwin Nikolais, and dance. The gift of grit and a sense of adventure supported my innocent, curious wanderings in a field for which I was totally unprepared.

Without a doubt, I came to the master teacher Alwin Nikolais "culturally deprived." Although I was a senior in college, I knew little of the arts and less about dance as an art. Still, I was innocently blessed in not knowing or appreciating the effect the deprivation had had on my development. The influence of my native Slavonic roots gave me confidence in the belief that everyone dances. It comes naturally. What's to learn?

What, then, did I bring to this school of creative dance? What made me stay? What strength did I have that I could use? What weaknesses did I have to overcome? The greatest strength, unrealized at the time, was my neuromuscular facility for performing complex movement patterns. I saw movement rapidly and in detail. I was able to pick up phrases easily. I had a good movement memory and could duplicate and retain elaborate patterns. This served me in good stead when I was invited to join the company. But at the beginning, I had no strength or technique to fully take advantage of my natural ability to move.

I was a workaholic and had a tolerance for hard knocks, bruises, aches, and pains and a dogged determination not to quit. This sustained me while I juggled teaching in the public high schools, taking classes to earn a master's degree, and learning about professional dance as a member of the Alwin Nikolais Dance

Company. What I brought to the playhouse those early years were a few possibilities, a number of inadequacies, and an overloaded schedule.

Nikolais was a man of extraordinary talent and artistry who was patient, tolerant, and willing to work with young people of varied levels of skill and talent. I was a beginner to dance. He was beginning to direct and organize a school and a company. He met his challenges and suffered or allowed us time while he tested his theories of movement and creativity on a small group of dancers. He proved that he was a master teacher/artist as we developed and began to demonstrate his theories of creativity through dance. He shared the value of art in life with the possibility of living life with art.

Nikolais continues as a creative legacy. This essay is a tribute to him and to the "Nikolais tradition," which is a carefully coined phrase that represents for me his school of teaching and choreography. He had his personal choreographic vision. However, the dance technique he taught remained clearly objective, unstylized, and unmannered. This is the foundation of the tradition exemplified by the organization, methods, and content of his teachings. He established a school of thought, not a studio of training. The curriculum of the school was divided into several major areas: technique or dance skill, theory of movement, composition of dance or choreography, and performance.

Nikolais taught technique through the use of concepts such as time, space, direction, levels, and dynamics, to name a few. Each concept was taught through specifically crafted movement experiences that the students were expected to master within the class time. When the phrases were successfully performed, an understanding of the concept was realized. The phrases were adapted to various levels of skill. Through practice, skill would be developed. Each class was a new challenge to further enhance skill and deepen understanding. Clarity of performance resulted from attention to the concept. The substance or essence of the movement was enriched with accuracy of articulation, unencumbered by manner or attitude.

Theory of movement was taught through improvisation. This presented an opportunity for each student to achieve an understanding of the concept of dance through individual creative investigation. With this method of teaching, permission was granted to explore one's personal creative direction. Through this objective approach to teaching technique, improvisation, composition, and performance, I came to define creativity for myself within very strict parameters. I believe that creativity requires fierce independence, uniqueness, and originality. Dance that evolves from this independence does not, and should not, fall into any one category or style, not even the Nikolais style, but should be a movement representation of the idea to be communicated. Nor should a concert of works be of a singular creative approach.

Dances should be baffling, yet communicative and should defy expectations, not standards. They should fall under no single label, yet cut across many; they should be nonrepetitive or reflective and be distinctly and thoroughly developed. Dancers who practice their art on the basis of these principles of independence are living up to the term *creative freedom* and are thereby true to the memory of the Nikolais tradition. Those who are establishing an independent and unique aesthetic, whose style is indefinable, and whose work is difficult to codify are functioning in the Nikolais tradition. Those who cause pigeonholers to cry in agony are functioning in the Nikolais tradition. Those who imitate him or who get caught up in any trendy imitation of any style have misunderstood the demand of creativity and have misunderstood the teaching of Alwin Nikolais. These are difficult expectations. But I believe they are appropriate standards. I have tried to be true to their spirit.

Nikolais taught principles of motion and concepts of creative investigation, and he instilled in us a desire for creative expression through motion. This was the foundation of information from which I developed my particular approach to teaching and choreographing. After leaving the company, I set out to implement the theories of the Nikolais tradition. I came to appreciate deeper levels of his intentions. I personalized and redirected the theories as I made my efforts as a fledgling artist, rejecting the trend of becoming an exemplary exponent of any single style.

Because I was interested in education and not training, because I wanted my dancers and students to demonstrate understanding through movement in conjunction with skills, and because my neuromuscular facility made complex movement patterns easy, I considered technique less important and understanding far more valuable. So I remembered, absorbed, and appreciated that which was compatible with my own creative inclination. I felt this was what he intended us to do. That was his legacy. For this, I am very grateful.

With the principles of motion as the basis for my teaching of dance technique, improvisation, and choreography, my objectivity was assured. I did not depend on myself as the focus of the movement materials that I taught. They were always based on the concepts.

Each student was a puzzle of ideas. Each presented with a complex series of physical needs that affected his or her ability to fulfill movement demands. To help each to succeed, my teaching became increasingly analytical and scientifically based. The concepts of movement were enlarged forms of the Nikolais tradition to which I added biomechanical and anatomical information. I felt I needed to know more about the structure of the body, the bones, joints, muscles, and nerves, and what part they played in learning the technique of dance. I found myself devising methods of teaching movement based on anatomical considerations. It fascinated me to realize that I could teach the same class to fifteen dancers and still take into account the anatomical differences of each without compromising skill for professional fulfillment.

The structure of the body has to be respected. Personal structural deviations of the teacher, such as an abnormal range of motion, should not be forced on all dancers. Neither should limitations of students or teachers be used as acceptable criteria for establishing style or skill. The students' bodies are the responsibility of the teacher. I take that responsibility seriously. Yet, the demands of creativity often expand the demands on the body. They call for a wider range of motion, a more complex configuration of movement materials. Increases in challenge through explosive interaction between dancers require more and more information about the body. New styles are pushing dancers' bodies. Open creative boundaries are pushing their physical structures off balance. These demands can be met safely through careful application of anatomical and biomechanical information. There is creative excitement in the requirement to apply new knowledge to find more challenging movement.

What a gift is enmeshed in the duty to care and be careful. What a vast source of creative movement choices can grow out of the decision to teach from an anatomical base. It need not be restrictive nor inhibit the flow of the class. Information from the field of motor learning forced me to address the conflict between the practice of technical training of dancers and the effort to guide dancers to their creative fulfillment. Each is a viable and separate program in the complete education of a dancer. Each, however, develops skills that need to be utilized depending upon the role the dancer is playing, whether performer or choreographer.

As we spend the predominant amount of time training students through repetitious drills of a set series of movements, they become skillful in performing that style of movement. This will return in the automatic use of this style for all requirements of dance—performing and creative. It is reasonable to expect that the creative work of these dancers will reflect the style in which they have been drilled. This is appropriate when the teacher is also the choreographer, who will be directing these young people to re-create his or her own choreography.

We need to spend an equal amount of time supporting the inventive ingenuity of dancers by giving them more opportunity to investigate a wider range of movement options. Exercises for creative classes, for example, need to be devised to block or inhibit the tendency to repeat learned movement patterns for every assignment. The goal should be to invent new combinations and styles of motion motivated by the idea or intention of the dance.

There is such a thing as an individual creative movement style. To find it requires work, with reason and purpose. To produce unique dance careers requires unfailing commitment. Schools of dance should offer opportunity and support for those who choose to follow the goal of creative freedom in movement. The Henry Street Playhouse School of Dance offered this opportunity. Nikolais was responsible for its development.

Nikolais gave the gift of a rich tradition. No matter how that tradition is utilized and personalized, we must acknowledge the gift. The gift lies in the unique approach to teaching dance as a means of encouraging creativity. Teaching itself is a creative activity. The tradition involves teaching creatively.

A gift given must be passed on. It becomes stronger as it is multiplied in the works of hundreds of students. They in turn will pass on the legacy in the greater demonstration of creativity. The Nikolais tradition was the impetus for me. The legacy is being passed on by many. We thank you, Nik, for preserving the right to our creative freedom.

9
Spontaneous Creation
(Dance Improvisation)

SHIRLEY RIRIE

During my sixty-plus years of dancing (yes, I still feel I am dancing all the time), dance improvisation has been my favorite place to be. There is a magic when you are completely in the moment of dance; your body is in tune with time, space, and energy; your spirit transcends any place you have been before; your emotional feeling state is connected; your mind is focused on the moment; and if you are dancing with someone else, the above sensations are replicated, and you both dance as one. I always said, "when I dance, I sense my livingness," and this happens more fully when an improvisation really clicks.

I remember, as a child, dancing around the living room when no one was home observing. I danced my heart out, and the feeling was glorious. You find this kind of love of dancing in untrained dancers or beginners. Once technique is introduced and the focus is on "doing the movement correctly," that joy of dancing sometimes leaves for awhile, and with it the freedom, abandon, and spontaneity of improvisation also leaves. So, the dancer's quest is to keep the freshness of spirit alive while training in the technicalities of the body machine.

I was lucky in my training. My college teacher and mentor, Elizabeth Hayes, believed in teaching improvisation side by side with technique and composition classes; and because I had a natural predilection for approaching dance improvisationally, this was the most natural approach for me. I remember trying to improvise in my ballet classes as a child and getting a royal drubbing. Next, I was fortunate to study with Alwin Nikolais and Anna Halprin. Each of them approached the improvisation process in an entirely different way, and from each I received great gifts. Nikolais used improvisation as the way to understand the theory of dance deeply and by experience. I remember finding myself transformed as I became bigger than life in a "kookie kabuki" problem with him. Graining is something my body knows through his careful tutelage.

A term coined by Nikolais, *graining* means directing the attention of the audience to a particular point in the body by means of focus and energy, much as the grain of a piece of wood focuses one's eye to the core. I also discovered his concept of *gestalt*, which has stayed with me throughout my dancing life as a beacon that answers my questions as I choreograph and perform. A German word meaning "whole," *gestalt* has no exact counterpart in English. For a dancer, it means the movement is executed as if it fits the dancer in an organic way, as if it belongs, and the theme of the dance is organic to the total composition. Each movement belongs to the theme, and the theme develops with no extraneous material. In Gestalt therapy, the whole is both the figure and the ground, which in dance terms would mean the body and the space that surrounds it, or as we sometimes say, positive space (the body) and negative space (the space surrounding the body). The whole can include music, movement, costumes, and lighting. As you can see, this very encompassing term takes concentrated study to fully understand. The easiest way to identify the gestalt is through shape, motion, or mood.

With Halprin, I happened on dance ideas that were later developed into choreography, such as a very funny improvisation with folding screens called "Screen Test," and a solo piece using Barlach sculptures as a stimulus that turned into many dances. My most profound experience with Halprin was a night on her outdoor dance deck that elicited a group improvisation incorporating the voice and a sense of soaring. The audience was struck dumb in silence afterwards, and we knew we had soared. We also knew we had made "art." For me, it was the highest moment of "becoming" in a dance. The spontaneous moment of creation and performance came together for the whole group in a totally connected way, and it was fully received by the audience, which became part of the creative spirit that was present for the performers. Because I had that strong improvisation experience, the memory never left me, and my goal as an artist and a teacher was to have this kind of moment happen again in my life and in the life of my students. I was carried to new heights of possibility.

I think most dancers improvise when they create movement for class or choreography. With some, the movement initiates intellectually; with others, it comes more intuitively. But always there are times when the body takes over, and the exploration is experimental and playful. This is the creative process at work, and for the improviser, it is the heart of creativity.

I like to work with my dancers in an improvisational way when I choreograph. If I am able to motivate them to catch the spirit of what I am trying to do, I find their contributions to be fresh and illuminating to me. I am led to new territories. I am stimulated to explore further, and they are rewarded by being more involved in the creation of the work. The choreography then becomes a true collaboration, and because of their investment, the dancers understand the material and the concept of the piece and can bring this understanding and a knowledge to the performance that goes far beyond the usual method of learning movement without such a personal investment.

A friend once came to me after a concert and said, "I would like to get inside your head to see where all your ideas come from. Each dance you make seems to come from a new, unique place." I told her of the advantage of being open to collaboration with your dancers and how that facilitates the imaginative results. Also, the product, the performance, has a depth. The dancers become more involved because of their shared experience in creation.

Teaching improvisation is a delicate process. The teacher must be sensitive to each happening. Knowing when and how much to talk or to coach is imperative. If one says something at the wrong moment, the flow of the improvisation might stop dead. On the other hand, just the right word of encouragement or the suggestion to try something specific might be all that is needed to get a group to connect. Concentration is the key here, and the knack of heightening the concentration level for those who improvise is the goal.

An improvisation session needs to be set up properly. The student needs to be ready in mind, body, and spirit for the work ahead. A gifted teacher can provide the conditions for that readiness. If the student is prepared in mind and body and motivated in spirit, there is almost a guarantee of success in solving the improvisation problem.

You might set a mood and a behavioral attitude. Getting the dancer into the moment and challenged by the concept is necessary. If you can create a gestalt where everything fits and makes sense, you enhance the clarity of the idea. The clearer the concept, the movement, and the use of time, space, and energy, the greater the chance you and the audience have of knowing if the improvisation works. Once this kind of clarity is achieved, the dance starts making itself. It is as if you, the dancer, are part of a great organic whole, and the choices you make become automatic.

This may begin to sound like a bunch of mumbo jumbo or magic. But, indeed, there is magic in a good improvisation. We understand that the "goodness," the success, is coming from the organic rightness of all that is happening. There needs to be absolute authenticity in everything the dancer does. "This is me dancing." "No one else will do it exactly like I do it in this time and place." The dancer needs to be open, to have the ability to take risks. Men and boys do very well in the improvisational setting; they have the physical daring and interest in throwing their bodies around, which is one of the reasons contact improvisation has such success among them. There is no reason women and girls cannot be risk takers, and many of them are. They often have a longer background in technical training, so they have the capacity to articulate the body in infinite and subtle ways.

The mixing it up of all kinds of dancers in improvisation sessions allows for borrowing and trading of movement experiences. I have often seen a dancer with limited technical skill perform in improvisation with a very skilled, advanced dancer and match the performance in such a way that both were brilliant. This is a possibility when you improvise well; many limits are erased, and the potential is there for magnificence.

We once held a workshop consisting of seven ten-hour marathon weekends. Thirty of the participants were skilled, professional artists and teachers in dance, and the other forty were classroom teachers ranging from kindergarten to college instructors. Most of what we did was improvisation, and the mix was great. The classroom teachers became dancers both as creators and as performers. All of us learned a huge amount about ourselves, about dance, and about each other. My point in telling about this workshop is that the skill level had no bearing on the outcome of the sessions. Certainly, the presence of skilled dancers added a potential level of success and a lot of inspiration. But the unskilled people were equally successful in coming up with remarkable solutions to improvisation problems.

All too often, there is no teacher available who understands the challenging task of leading improvisation. Much can be done by forming a group that improvises together. Joan Woodbury and I created a video series to help teachers or students lacking knowledge of this important and necessary part of dance. With the videos and the explanatory book, a person could become proficient in improvising over time.

Working in the public schools with dance improvisation is very rewarding. Children on the elementary level are very apt and familiar with the improvisational form. The way they play with their friends, creating imaginary scenarios, making up games, and fantasizing, is really improvisation. Developing the imagination is crucial to the education of the child; also, physical and social interaction is motivating. I find great enthusiasm and involvement in the improvisational process when I work with children. To my mind, dance improvisation should be an important, basic part of the education of every child on the elementary level. Edwin Foshay, an important education generalist, listed six attributes that define what it means to be human: physical, mental, social, emotional, aesthetic, and spiritual. He says that learning should be balanced among these traits. Dance can give strong practice in each of these areas—and I may add, very few subjects hit all six attributes. We talk about training children in "higher-level thinking"; this means we teach them to be effective with the creative process, to think for themselves, to make judgments. This happens every time we give children a problem to solve. In dance, solving problems, finding new, creative ways to put movement together, and performing studies for classmates that are evaluated on the spot by peers all contribute to practice in creativity, higher-level thinking, and socialization. All six Foshay traits are in constant practice when children are solving dance problems. Creating a dance in a group is a perfect way to learn how to work productively with others.

Children can create a dance study in one thirty- to forty-five-minute class period, if the skills of improvisation are available. It is exciting to get together with a group of classmates to make a dance. The successful teacher knows that the lead-up to this process must provide resources for the problem solving. The concept of the problem to be solved must be fully understood. This can happen through improvising with the material. Say the problem is to work with straight and curved lines. First, the class might improvise to find interesting body shapes where only straight lines are permitted. What are the possibilities? See them, comment on the aesthetics of the shapes. Which ones do you like the best, and why? Can you create a two-person, straight-lined shape? (This immediately becomes a social interaction). Can a straight-lined shape exist in the air for a moment? (A physical challenge). Make a sequence of four shapes that progress from one to another, with straight-lined transitions, and then do the same backwards. (A mental challenge). Do the same exploring with curved shapes. Make straight-lined floor patterns and curved floor patterns. Make a combination of straight and curved patterns. Can you travel on a floor pattern with your curved and straight-lined shapes, making strong contrasts between straight and curved? This introduction of resources will lead to eventual composition.

Studies can be quickly improvised within a group to show ideas that are then evaluated as to the success of solving the problem. Also, aesthetics are always an issue when watchers give feedback. If you provide possible music selections to use as a basis for the studies, it is easier for the children to get to a place where emotional feeling states enter into the process. Music is a good avenue for putting feeling into the performance of the movement. Identifying the possible feeling states suggested by the music will help. But always remember that each individual has different emotional and aesthetic responses. Be sure to talk about that, and be sure the class learns to respect individual differences. The emotional and spiritual aspects of this series of lessons will probably arrive out of the group dance that is eventually performed. When I talk about the spiritual side of dance, it is when all aspects come together, and you realize that a moment of transcendence has occurred. You have become more. This means you discovered the quality of the motion for yourself, you jumped higher than you have ever jumped before, you connected with another dancer in a successful way. The spiritual and emotional sides of dance are closely linked. We know through scientific studies that our emotions are tied to physical movement. When we leap across the floor in a dance class, there is pure joy manifested in the act. When that leap soars in a way it has never soared before, when we feel that soaring completely in both a kinesthetic and an emotional way, we may have a spiritual moment. I want all children to have the experience of feeling their body moving in this physical, emotional, and spiritual way. It is possible.

Because improvising studies for classmates is so easy once the fundamentals are learned, performances can be prolific. I have found in my teaching career that performance is where the life change experiences happen for students. It is when you put yourself on the line and show others, that you realize important things about yourself and about how you are working. You also learn about the problem you are solving, and you discover ways to do it better. I encourage many improvised performances with attentive audiences. This makes learning fun, productive, and motivating. These performances can lead up to more choreographed and practiced dances. Certainly, a sense of accomplishment comes when you have rehearsed and become proficient at what you perform. But often, the length of the class day does not provide a lot of time for practice. So I tend to work more with improvisational performance in the elementary grades. An after-school group that is highly motivated will benefit from more serious rehearsal and choreography.

Even though improvisation has been my "lifeblood" through my years of dance, I remember times when I felt very uncomfortable and unwilling to participate. I needed motivation and atmosphere as much as the beginners in the group. I also remember some very wonderful and crazy times when I, too, was a student or when my class of students went "over the top." One such time, I was improvising with two other dancers in front of a group of high school students, on a large scaffold doing a "line of action" improvisation in which we used lines of dialogue and props supplied by the audience. These dances were usually funny, but this one time the text and the relationship were deadly serious. This experience made me realize that an improvisation often finds its own form and content, and one must not go into the act of improvisation with a definite expectation of the outcome. Another time, in the late 1960s, during the days of the "free university," a group of behavioral scientists, English professors, dancers, and other faculty had some deeply revealing sessions in an experimental improvisation class that went on for a full quarter. None of the men were dancers, and many of the women were; for both groups, the sessions were profound. Movement improvisation is a great leveler. Technical skills are only a part of what a person brings to class; remembering Foshay's traits, all those aspects of the person are functioning, and wonderful things happen when human beings function together in a creative art process, using bodies, imagination, physical movement, and all the rest.

For many years, I taught advanced improvisation on Wednesday evenings for three hours straight every spring quarter. Some people came to the class year after year. It was a wonderful time to focus. No interruptions, and lots of time to get into depth with the problem. Bobby McFerrin accompanied this class one year, and he subsequently told me that much of his later vocal improvisation came out of the release of these sessions. A music major who now does film scores in Hollywood was another one of these students, and though he was a musician, not a dancer, he was a huge catalyst to creative work. Going to that optimal place, dancing in ways you never thought possible, executing physical feats that could not be done in another circumstance, creating partner lifts, and defying gravity—all these events and many more evolve from the focused concentration, heightened perception, and clear spontaneity of good improvisation.

Do it.

10
Adventures in Real Space: An Alternate Mode of Thinking and Problem Solving

MICHAEL HOEYE

What can creativity offer students as a method of decision making? Creative work is physical and pragmatic. Engagement and accountability are its hallmarks—not self-absorption or idle freedom. Creativity is a form of problem solving that uses time and logic differently than traditional analytical thinking. It is a continuum of computations, assessments, and adjustments in which solutions evolve through time. Creativity uses thinking itself differently, linking it much more closely to action of some sort. This is its value in teaching decision making. Real-life decisions have outcomes. Outcomes affect lives.

Here is a simple classroom exercise that uses movement to train students in the essential, decision-making processes of creative work: The setting is an unobstructed space like a gymnasium or a conference room. Students are randomly paired. Each member of a pair is assigned the role of leader or follower. The follower is blindfolded. The partners work facing each other, with arms extended comfortably forward, hands meeting palm-to-palm. The position is neutral. It favors neither partner. Conversation is not permitted. Communication is strictly through physical contact.

The assignment to the leader is to move the follower through space in a manner that provides an enjoyable kinesthetic experience, keeping the follower clear of physical danger, monitoring and avoiding the other pairs moving through the same space, and using music as an indicator of pace and rhythm. The assignment to the follower is to pay attention and keep up.

Music simplifies the situation by providing a framework of possibilities for rhythm and tempo. It also functions as an external reality that must be accommodated. For beginners, I use a well-known pop standard with an easy, walkable beat and a simple, recognizable style such as big band, country and western, or Latin. After the first round, the partners change roles, and the exercise is repeated. After the second round, the pairs change partners.

A QUESTION OF LEADERSHIP

The challenge to the leader is to step out into an unpredictable flow of events and to respond to it by assembling and communicating streams of information and instructions that combine the variables of direction, velocity, and duration. This is the palette of decision-making possibilities that the leader can variously combine to move the follower pleasurably through an exploration of unknown and invisible space.

The value of this experience from a management or decision-making view-point is that simplistic either/or thinking is irrelevant. Variables must each be determined and expressed precisely. They must be determined and expressed in real time to meet emergent events. And because decisions must be comprehended and executed by the blindfolded partner, clear communication is critical.

Each of the leader's decisions initiates a series of consequences that limit or expand the possibilities of what can follow. Each choice is followed instantly by another choice. In this context, momentum becomes a determining factor—a critical variable in its own right. Real-life decisions create momentum that is as real, if not as palpable, as the physical momentum the students experience on the floor. Momentum is ambivalent. It gives, and it takes away. It is a foundation to be built upon or an obstacle to be overcome.

Momentum has a profound effect upon an individual's or an organization's ability to cope with change. Momentum is a concrete reality in this exercise. It forces the leader to account for the effects of his or her past decisions and to begin to understand decision making in the context of continuous flow rather than isolated events.

FOLLOW THE LEADER

In this exercise, as in most of life, the quality of the follower often determines the ability of the leader. Following is a highly alert state of attention, the goal of which is to interpret, extend, and amplify the intention of the leader. It is the art of implementing decisions.

The first challenge for the follower is to isolate and override his or her own movement impulses in order to present a neutral but actively mobile instrument to the leader. The second is to pay close attention to the push and pull of the leader's hands. With the eyes closed, the hands are the only reliable sources of information and instruction. It is the follower's responsibility to track the sequence of instructions and to interpret them accurately, immediately, and with appropriate amplification.

Following is an action of appropriate response. People are surprised to discover that following is not related to passivity. A certain degree of resistance is required in order to accurately interpret instructions. But it is not passive resistance. Nor is it emotional resistance. Following demands an active, self-conscious, physical presence combined with a willingness to move. The follower must manifest this by assuming a navigable posture. The hands and arms must serve as a steering mechanism for the body. They must be connected to the whole. Resistance is used to transmit momentum rather than absorbing or dampening it. This is a new experience for most students. Searching for the optimal navigational stance is a question of making small adjustments in resistance and tension and evaluating the results. It means paying close attention to a narrow band of experience. It requires the same sort of nuanced evaluation that leading requires. And it brings with it the same degree of accountability. For many people, this highly focused state of attention is an absorbing experience—very often described as euphoric. This euphoric quality is related to the mental concentration of play and flow.

Assessing the situation. After each partner has had a turn at leading and following, the partners change. This is a good time for a short explanation of the exercise in terms of information flow, for identifying the variables that the information addresses, and for discussing some of the problems that have been encountered.

The possibilities in a nutshell. The truth is, the possibilities don't fit in a nutshell. They are infinite. By working with a number of partners, all students begin to get a sense of their own strengths and limitations as both leaders and followers. They also get hands-on experience with other leaders and followers. They begin to develop a picture of the skills and responsibilities of both positions and to learn to cope strategically with the variations they encounter. They are often surprised to see themselves more clearly.

Nobody's perfect. The first thing you learn in this exercise is that you have a lot to learn when it comes to being a leader or a follower. The second thing you learn is that you can learn it. Humor plays an important part to defuse performance anxieties. Here are some thumbnail sketches of some of the foibles of both leaders and followers broken down by type:

The leaders

- believe they are born to lead. Hyperactive, oblivious leaders gush volumes of baroque instructions that leave their partners stumbling in the dust. They picture themselves as dynamic leaders. The problem, they insist, lies in the follower.
- jump to conclusions. Reactionary leaders revert to pump-handle cartoons of remembered social dances, avoiding altogether the uncertainty and anxiety of original exploration and plummeting rapidly into the tedium of social charade.
- turn the tables. Passive-aggressive leaders natter about anxiously, baiting their followers into motion that gives the erstwhile leader something to follow.

The followers

- never miss a beat. Unfortunately, it's the wrong drummer. These are self-deluding leaders camouflaged as followers—a fascinating approach. They are persons who pride themselves on being cooperative. And they are co-operative to the extent that the leaders accept the rigid framework within which they are willing to work. Unfortunately, the framework overdetermines the outcome.
- are waiting for their Pygmalion. Basically, these are dead batteries waiting for a charge. They require not just direction but a continuous input of energy and revert to absolute inertia from moment to moment as visions of potential puppet masters dance in their heads.
- suffer from rag-doll selflessness. They are too willing to be able; limp noodles that absorb direction rather than respond to it and overly coopera-tive. All things are possible, but nothing seems to happen. They are masters of smiling sabotage.

Searching for ideals. It doesn't take much effort trying to follow a poor leader before a clear image of an effective leader emerges: Start slow, build smoothly. Clearheaded leaders assess the music, map the room, monitor their partner, and begin to lay out simple lines through space that the follower can respond to. The movement grows in complexity as the leader and the follower grow in confidence.

The same holds true for an effective follower: Willing and able—a careful observer. Definite occupant of space. Capable of sustained attention. Curious and willing participant who can analyze and amplify events on the fly.

Accountability is the point of this whole exercise. The basic structure of this exercise is a feedback loop between the leader and the follower. The leader is accountable for decisions because he or she is physically bound to their effects. The follower is accountable for responsiveness because the clarity and amplification of his or her responses convey accurate feedback to the leader. The result is a learning community composed of two people, capable of adapting to circumstances, formulating goals, and testing methods for achieving them. Their performance offers a fairly accurate, moment-to-moment illustration of their abilities to concentrate on the skills of leading or following.

The truth of the matter is that most of us are all over the map when it comes to either. We lack practice at sustaining or developing them. We lack adequate language for describing the nuances of leading and following. We lack methods for observing the actual processes involved. We lack tools for modulating the effects of culture, gender, personality, and individual history on our abilities to both lead and follow. For a society that increasingly operates on the basis of managing behavior, we lack the essential disciplines of managing and being managed.

A matter of empathy. The partnered-movement improvisation of this exercise is empathic or dysfunctional. Information and instructions either flow between the partners or they don't. In order for there to be flow, discrete moments of listening and evaluation must alternate with moments of instructing or responding. If empathy occurs, it may take one of two forms: static or dynamic.

First steps first. The first goal of this exercise is static empathy, which maintains clearly defined, unchanging roles for each of the partners. In that sense, it resembles traditional social dancing, but unlike social dancing, we are not bound by gender roles. It is important that students experience both roles and learn to differentiate the skills involved in sustaining each of them. Also unlike traditional social dancing, there are no predetermined styles or sequences of steps. Except for maintaining clear communication and navigation between the two partners, there are no predefined outcomes. No right or wrong. In that sense, this is a realistic management problem.

But that's not the end of it. Dynamic empathy exists when the roles of instructing and responding are not the exclusive domain of either partner but alternate according to some internal rhythm. The alternation in roles may be as definite as black and white, or it may be graded in indeterminate percentages. The result is not necessarily mathematical equality. One partner may dominate the directorial process. But dynamic empathy means that the balance of leadership is not predetermined by decree. It is continually adjusted by the partners as they monitor the flow of events and attempt to optimize their performance. In dynamic empathy, the identity of the leader may not be immediately apparent to the partners or to an observer. It may also not be relevant to the quality of the performance. In fact, this fluid state of empathy represents a higher level of management thinking that is capable of faster and more optimal responses.

This is the kind of behavior that one reads about regularly under the rubrics of "leaderless organization" and "team management." This exercise offers an avenue for achieving this state in a relatively short amount of time. It serves as ongoing practice for both leadership and implementation. By studying both roles, students can learn to exercise each modality effectively and to make transitions between the two smoothly and consciously.

11

Putting It Together: Integrating the Arts in Learning and Living

CAROL NORTH

I am a theater artist. No, wait. I'm a teacher. Actually, I *could* say I'm a writer. But perhaps I'm really an administrator. No, let me start again. I am a former dancer. Well, the truth is, I am more of a singer and an actor, with a penchant for physical work. However, now my artistic work centers on directing rather than performing. But to be honest with you, I am an English major with a lifetime teaching certificate. (What sense does *that* make!) Okay, here's the gospel truth: *I am a casserole*. In a world in which everyone else seems to be a specialist, I am not. Once sheepish about that fact, now that I'm over fifty, I find it easier simply to admit what I am and get on with my work.

Fortunately, my professional life permits me to put all my ingredients together. In fact, my job mandates that I perform alchemy on a daily basis. I am the artistic director of Metro Theater Company, a professional theater that commissions, develops, produces, and tours new work for young people and families. Perhaps more than any of the performing arts, theater is the quintessential tapestry that weaves language, movement, music, and three-dimensional design. My responsibility to Metro combines education with theater. As an artist/educator, I work principally with teachers in professional development programs designed to help educators put the arts in their classrooms on a regular basis, as a way of thinking, teaching, learning. It simply makes sense to me, though it was by no means my experience in school.

Is this scenario familiar to you? Desks in rows. Students in desks. Bulletin boards, designed by the teacher, highlight the season of the year and only the best samples of students' work. All curriculum subject areas are taught separately. We spend an hour on reading, an hour on arithmetic, an hour on spelling and writing practice, an hour on science, and an hour on social studies. Sometime during the week, we have a gym class for exercise and team sports, all competitive. Lunch time. Play time is reserved for recess.

New scenario: high school and college. Maintain the previous description but change the names of the learning blocks from reading to "Modern British Novel"; arithmetic changes to calculus. Of course, the time devoted to play all but disappears. Sitting and listening time increases dramatically. Talking and writing are more formalized. At the end of my formal education, I receive a piece of paper that pronounces me valid. I am a grown-up with a degree who can and *does* get a job. After all, I am a good student. I am well behaved. I can sit still and be quiet for long periods of time. My handwriting is neat and tidy. I spell correctly. I organize my thoughts well on paper. Even when I don't study very much, I can guess my way through a multiple-choice test. I keep my course assignments neatly separated, just as the curriculum imposes its artificial boundaries. I love notebook dividers. No surprise, I chose to perpetuate the system and become a teacher. I lasted one year in public schools.

I wish I had been able to weave together all my passions when I was younger, when I was careening from compartment to compartment of my life, as if it were necessary to keep separate the life threads that naturally come together to form the tapestry of who I am. It took another ten years following my short hurrah with teaching to stumble into the place where I found my life's work. With Metro Theater Company, I found an artistic home in which my disparate elements could not only find their place but could expand and develop.

I am grateful to a handful of people who showed me the possibility of what I wish to call "full learning" and influenced the path my own life's work has taken. While I was teaching English my first year in Guilford, Connecticut, I had the good fortune to hear John Holt speak at Yale University. He sounded a well-timed wake-up call for me that afternoon with his lecture based on his best-selling book, *How Children Fail.*[1] I was deeply moved. Moreover, I was moved to action. I marched into the principal's office at Guilford Senior High School and told my boss I wanted to conduct an experiment with my classes for the following quarter. I wanted to assure all my students that no one would receive less than a C for the quarter, even if they sat on their fannies and did nothing. However, anyone could earn a higher grade by contracting with me and completing a specific body of work. I would assist them like a travel agent, recommending specific reading, critiquing their writing, engaging with them in discussion and reflection. I wanted to place primary responsibility for learning in my students' hands. Remarkably, my principal agreed to the plan.

It was a fascinating quarter. A few of the kids, exhausted by junior research papers in other classes, took me at my word and enjoyed a breather. The most profound impact, however, was on the handful of students who for the first time in their lives were told they could earn a B or even an A. Sixteen-year-old Jesse was one of those kids. He had been homeschooled by his father because they traveled extensively. His spelling was atrocious, and he was an odd social misfit, but he had a genuinely curious mind. He seized the opportunity to engage meaningfully and successfully in learning and earned a B. Thirty years later, I look back with wonder on the audacity of my first-year teacher's request and the support I received from Bill Clancy for my "John Holt experiment." Clancy encouraged me to make a change and wished me well as I tried.

My second debt of gratitude I pay to significant "life" teachers, my daughters Megan and Emily. They didn't know it at the time, of course, but I learned a profound lesson with them about instinctual, physical knowing. Gratefully, I approached motherhood by choice. I read lots of books in preparation. When I gave birth to Megan, all the book learning in the world didn't matter. Suddenly, *dramatically,* I was blessed with the wisdom of my body. I knew what to do, with the deepest kind of knowing. My body spoke to me with clarity and resonance. The power of that experience stays with me in my relationship to every aspect of my lifework.

My body led me, I think, to the next significant chapter in my learning. I discovered again a passion for dance that had tried to call to me when I was twelve but that was thwarted by ballet classes in which I felt painfully disconnected. While my daughters were toddlers, I found my way to a modern dance class. One thing led to another, until I actually signed up for classes on a regular basis at Webster University. With the urging of my husband, I auditioned for, and was accepted in, the Webster Dance Theatre. The choreography was difficult for me. I attributed it to my obvious lack of technique, until I took a master class with Merce Cunningham and another with members of the Nikolais Dance Theatre. Suddenly, something made sense in my body. Here was movement that possessed physical logic. I could *do* this! With a new sense of confidence, I signed up for a three-week intensive dance institute at Washington University taught by Phyllis Lamhut. I believe that's when I began dancing for the first time.

During the institute, Annelise Mertz offered me the opportunity to take her classes at Washington University. My relationship with this extraordinary woman, artist, and teacher began that day. For several years, I took as many classes as I could with various members of the department and with guest artists—technique, improvisation, and composition. The highlight was always the 4:00–6:00 P.M. beginner class that Mertz taught. Thirty to forty people filled the studio. The group was comprised of awkward newcomers to dance as well as advanced students who thrived on class time with this master teacher. Some were intimidated. I felt myself soar.

What was it that opened for me in this relationship? Mertz helped me understand that movement involves the entire person at this *very* moment in time. Nothing can be held back. The eyes, the ears, the mind, the imagination, the muscles, bones, organs, blood, and skin—*all* are vital to the dancer's presence. It was the most alive I had ever felt. I was present. I felt smart. I was entirely engaged in what I was doing, and what I was doing was continually stretching me to do more. I had never before felt so connected to my own learning.

Mertz inspired and challenged me as a teacher. She also led me to Metro Theater Company, which has been my artistic home for more than twenty years. I guess I tipped my hand with her in the compositions I created, which tended to be theatrical. She told me one day, "Metro Theater—I think this is for you." Right she was. I took three-year-old Megan with me to see the company's *Rootabaga Vaudeville Show.* We both danced out of the theater. I saw onstage a delightful fusion of dance, sound, music, language, wit, and story. I learned later that the company was committed to education, too. The only remaining piece was to get the job! It took two more years, but in 1977 I had the good fortune to be hired by founding artistic director Zaro Weil when she was rebuilding the ensemble. Good friends Branislav Tomich and Suzanne Costello were hired that year, too, along with a wonderful redheaded musician named Peter Hesed and a guy named Nick Kryah, whom I wasn't sure I liked very well. I married him fourteen years later.

As soon as we began rehearsing my first Metro production, *Somersault,* I realized I was in the place I wanted to be professionally. Everything about our work together came as a huge sigh of relief. I was finally engaged in the process of putting together all those things that had been kept separate artificially my entire life. The experience was a powerful affirmation of something within me that I couldn't name then.

Nearly twenty years later, I found the Rosetta stone that has helped me name that personal learning truth. Quite by coincidence, my path as an artist/educator crossed with the path of learning specialist Anne Powell. We were brought together in Winston-Salem, North Carolina, to plan and implement a series of professional development workshops for teachers. I had been working with teachers for several years in a program called "Integrating the Arts." Metro had enjoyed considerable success with this yearlong program, taught in partnership with Maryville University, including three years' funding from the National Endowment for the Arts. I knew intuitively and experientially that when teachers are engaged as learners in creative work, they generate powerful connections with lively, effective methods to teach their core curriculum. The teachers' hands-on experience catalyzed their connections. I had seen teachers transformed personally as a result of our work together in this class I was teaching. I had a hunch about what was going on, but it was still difficult to decode.

Powell gave me the key to understanding why the classes I was offering teachers were so powerful, so enlivening, and most important, so *effective* as teaching/learning experiences. Powell's work continues that of her mentor, Dawna Markova, a pioneer in brain-based research and learning differences. Briefly, here is a short summary of the basis for their theoretical model: We all use auditory, visual, and kinesthetic tools to take in new information and to express both what we know and who we are in the world. Yet, our minds don't navigate the learning process in the same ways. In fact, according to Markova and Powell, there are six Personal Thinking Patterns that reflect the unique ways we take in, absorb, and apply information.[2] We have different learning needs as we attempt to concentrate, organize, and store learning. We may be comfortable with some modes of expression, such as eye contact, speaking aloud, and physical contact and distinctly *less* so with others. You have your own examples from life; here are a few of mine.

- It drives me crazy to have music playing in the office, yet music helps our office manager feel more alert.
- I have always found accurate spelling a snap; my husband spells the same word differently every time he writes it.
- I get overwhelmed with the task of packing; but Nick has a particular genius for finding the right place for each object that must fit in the back of the van.
- Most of my classmates in school (or so I thought) enjoyed playing softball; I was always terrified during the game because I wasn't "physical." However, in the privacy of my living room, I could dance like nobody's business!

What I had been offering teachers in my professional development workshops were multiple ways of experiencing new learning and multiple ways to express what they learned. All were arts based. I used movement, drama, music, and visual design. We combined written and oral work with physical exploration. I gave the teachers the opportunity to be expressive with their curriculum. The

result? They had fun. They laughed. They felt alive. They made new connections. They took the approach back to their classrooms and reported that their
students were learning more effectively, and they themselves were not working as hard. Behavior problems lessened because the kids who were likely to
"act up" had a positive, challenging outlet for their physical energy.

Am I trying to make classroom teachers into artists? Certainly not. I am
inviting teachers to tap into the ways artists use movement, sound, drama, and
design to enliven the human experience. All the senses—the heart, the mind,
the soul—are called upon when we engage in art. The entire person longs to
be involved in learning. The arts offer the means to full engagement. And when
anything less is offered, a part of us simply checks out.

I look back again on my own schooling. How many hours did I spend with
only partial engagement—the minimum required? And what were those rare
and wonderful occasions when I really connected with a teacher and the learning that teacher was offering me? What made the difference? When I got excited about school, the learning held a kind of vitality, full of passion, movement, drama, and color, just like life! I remember "full learning" experiences
that invited my imagination to flower. My senses were fully engaged. I got excited about learning when the many languages of the body, including my emotions, were speaking and listening.

What gives me hope for the future, despite the conservative climate in our
country and the hue and cry of "Back to basics!" is that schools and teacher-
training programs are embracing a more holistic approach to teaching and learning. Lots of classrooms I enter now evidence a richer learning environment in
which students are invited to be lively "explorers" rather than passive vessels
in which to pour information. Let me share examples of some of the lively learning that I have witnessed in public schools. The work of these teachers is wor-
thy of celebration.

Karen teaches fourth grade in St. Joseph, Missouri. She turned the water cycle
into a simple song to a familiar tune, "I've Been Working on the Railroad."
The song had a series of gestures and physical actions that played out the natural
phenomena. Students especially enjoyed the accelerando: "Then it starts to rain,
then it starts to rain. . . ." Her students remembered the scientific facts of the
cycle months later through the auditory and muscle memory of that experience.

Judy teaches middle school mathematics in Hollister, Missouri. After struggling for years to make geometry more fun, she came up with a collaborative
approach to practicing the various sorts of triangles. Groups of three to four
students received a ball of string and instructions to build scalene, isosceles, and

equilateral triangles using their bodies and all the string. Gathering necessary information as they went, the groups proceeded to make triangles that scaled the walls of the classroom. Motivation was high because the assignment was both challenging and fun. Learning was effective. Test scores proved it.

Mary teaches high school history in Columbia, Missouri. With skeptical colleagues watching dubiously, she orchestrated a creative drama and movement event that brought to life the tensions of people occupying the fertile crescent in the Middle East. In groups of twenty, the students traveled from the mountains, over the sea, and across the desert to satisfy their fundamental need for fresh water. As each subsequent group tried to get water, the crowding intensified, their beliefs clashed, and the tensions mounted. Mary had given them a tangible experience that brought to life a facet of history that can seem remote in a textbook.

Greg teaches high school biology in Green City, Missouri. Because his students chronically had trouble understanding the role and function of the minute components of the cell, he decided to try something new in his unit on cellular biology. He assigned a three-dimensional design project that required the students to construct a cell out of the most imaginative materials they could think of. He required that students write a poem or short story from the point of view of one of the cell parts to demonstrate that they truly understood the relationships among the components. He was astonished at the creativity and the demonstrated understanding of his students' responses. Particularly surprising were the artful projects of students who had shown no academic interest previously.

These examples are so simple. No elaborate productions nor costly materials were necessary. Yet every project or lesson was not only fun for students and teachers but also successful. The curriculum came alive using basic elements of drama, movement, design, and creative writing. These teachers put it together with their curriculum once they had had the arts experience themselves.

My fourteen-month-old granddaughter Anna knows how to put it together, too. I am taking my lessons from her these days. Anna is the very essence of vibrant motion, fueled by curiosity and wonder for the world she inhabits. Her senses are all tuned in to the world she explores so hungrily. From time to time, she slows down her travel and gives close attention to a detail. The other day, she stopped to pick up the dried leaves of a plant that had fallen to the floor. Her focus sharpened, her fingers explored the crackled texture of the leaves, her voice downshifted into a growling motor sound as she examined the specimen. She lifted it for me to name. I told her it was a dried-up leaf. She handed it to me and was off again. The world is Anna's school. She moves through it, into it, on it, over it, learning as she goes its names, physical properties, delights, and dangers. Her journey is dramatic and always filled with creative movement. She greets the wind chimes on my porch each time she visits. Each time she hears them, the sound is delicately wondrous to her. We pore over the pages of her books again and again. Each time, the stories and images work their magic anew. What a model for professional actors with whom I work is this little one, who explores her world with a spontaneity that she creates again and again, even when the game is familiar. What a powerful reminder for me to witness the beauty of pure learning, which Anna appreciates so fully. There is no formal sequence or limited modality to her exploration. Anna takes the whole of herself into the whole of her learning all the time. That's my lifelong wish for her. That is the legacy I long to leave for other artists, for educators at every level, for all young people. That's my goal for myself in this dramatic dance I'm living. Have you ever seen a casserole dance? It's quite a sight.

NOTES

1. John Holt, *How Children Fail* (New York: Dell, 1971; Reading: Addison, Wesley, Longman, 1995).

2. See Dawna Markova, *The Open Mind: Exploring the Six Patterns of Natural Intelligence* (Berkeley: Conari, 1996); Dawna Markova and Anne Powell, *How Your Child Is Smart: A Life-Changing Approach to Learning* (Berkeley: Conari, 1992); and Dawna Markova and Anne Powell, *Learning Unlimited: Using Homework to Engage Your Child's Natural Style of Intelligence* (Berkeley: Conari, 1998).

12

Being (and Doing) in the Body

BRANISLAV TOMICH

"Using a mind/body/spirit integration approach, students will explore the physical and emotional self through a series of carefully guided exercises designed to create acute awareness; the goal of which is the use of the total self in creating an active, alive, and unselfconscious onstage presence in order to communicate effectively, efficiently, and effortlessly. Ultimately, participants will discover this work to be an empowerment tool for all aspects of life and living."

The previous paragraph is one that I composed for a university-level performing arts class. While it was originally written for that purpose, it is in fact the basic premise of every workshop, residency, or master class I teach. Though the material may vary, its essence does not.

My own background is an eclectic one. I include a bit of it here because it is fundamental to the evolution of the work that I am doing today. I received a degree in art education from Washington University in St. Louis. A series of drawings and paintings of dancers led me to make an extensive study of dance, movement, and bodywork. My passion and respect for movement awareness/education came from my relationship with my dance mentor, Annelise Mertz, at Washington University. I can only describe this association as one of the most exhilarating, inspiring, and enlightening ones of my life. The creation and performance of dance theater works led me to acting and ultimately to playwriting. It is the sum total of this journey, but specifically my movement base, that is the foundation of all of my work as an actor and a performing arts educator. Indeed, it is my belief that each of us brings our entire emotional, physical, intellectual, and spiritual self to each new moment.

In acting, we strive toward what is called "being in the moment" to re-create anew the same role that we may have been performing for months, and in some cases, years. How do we do that? I believe we do it by truly being in our body and completely in present time. Each breath a new one. Each moment a fresh one. And ideally, at the same time, with a mind and spirit open to that moment, and a body poised to act on it. Every thought, feeling, and emotion we experience is expressed in some form of action through this amazingly articulate instrument that we call our body. By *doing* in the body, I refer to any physical activity that is thus informed and therefore performed with heightened awareness. My desire as an actor is to examine and explore this instrument fully, in order that I might be totally aware of it and sensing it, thus gaining confidence and security through familiarity with my tools; the ultimate goal being that this awareness becomes second nature, enabling me to call upon it for assistance in an instant.

I have seen time and time again the value and success of movement education. I have seen this in a myriad of populations and in infinite variations of age, background, experience, and training. I have done the work described here with many populations, among them professional actors, dancers, and singers, college students, "at risk" youth (ages 9–12), teens, incarcerated juveniles, adult persons with HIV, senior citizens, nuns, educators, and other nonperforming adult professionals. I prefer to use the word *guide* when referring to my role in these situations, as I feel that I am there to share my collection of information while guiding the participants through the experience in a gentle and supportive environment. In all cases, I observed physical and emotional changes occurring right before my eyes. I share these concepts with you and invite you to use them if you find them to be congruent with what you are doing.

With each of these populations, my starting point was the same: the body, our innate physicality. Beginning first with stillness and by concentrating on not moving, on being perfectly still, we remind ourselves of the undeniable fact of our "movability." The movement sense. The urge to move. By paying attention to the internal movement of our bodily organs and rhythms, we are reminded that the movement within and without is a constant. By "listening" in this fashion, we increase our awareness of our body and embark on a deeper and more conscious exploration and observation of its (our) potential. Eureka! We rediscover it. It is my confirmed belief that this is empowering information.

In this essay, I focus on my work with incarcerated teens at a midwestern juvenile courts facility. This is a detention residence for juveniles awaiting court dates, primarily persons of color ranging in age from thirteen to seventeen. The reasons for their internment range from truancy to felonies and violent crimes. The outcome of their trials might include return to the custody of a parent or a guardian or transference to a state detention facility. So, I see them in this kind of "way station" on the road to whatever comes next. Will they make a change for the better and acknowledge the error of their ways, or will they go to deeper lockup? I see them once or twice per week for ninety minutes over a period of four to six weeks. They come to me restless, angry, frustrated, bored, and confused. I ask myself, "What can I possibly do?" I quickly acknowledge that I am merely a diversion. I'm that not-so-square guy who's going to teach them how to be actors. Or so they think. I must add here that prior to our first session, I performed an abbreviated version of my multi-character, one-man show in the combination cafeteria/assembly room. With state-of-the-art technology (read: boom box for my music tapes resting on a water cooler and glamorous fluorescent lunchroom lighting to illuminate my expressive actor's face) and the invaluable participation of my accompanist Knez Jakovac on mandolin, we attempted to entertain.

I'm looking at about sixty faces. They read curious, indifferent, annoyed. Behavior is orderly, almost rigid. Guards flank the walls. After all, these kids are incarcerated. The idea to provide the performance before the workshop was a conscious decision. I figured if I could hook them there, I'd have won the first round. It worked. Following the performance, I fielded questions, and the forum was opened up for communication. It might interest the reader to know that many of these questions referred to my physicality and to the visible changes they witnessed as I changed from character to character. They recalled, counting and describing, all ten of them. Looking out over this sea of youthful faces, what struck me most (and I mean struck) was the realization that whatever their crimes, whatever callousness or insensitivity they might possess, this was a roomful of youthful pain—kids in pain acting out by inflicting pain. I think that unconsciously I made the decision at that very moment to try to provide an experience that would focus on healing and the possibility of positive change. Volunteers were then selected for an acting class. My goal? To show up. To be myself. To be in the moment and to try (despite my obsessive-compulsive lesson plans) to simply pay attention. To listen. It's funny how we often forget the most basic communication skills in our efforts to *educate*. I tell them that there is no right or wrong in this work, only better choices. This is a new concept to many, if not all, of them. I eventually find myself repeating the phrase "Make a wholesome choice." And I state my definition of the word *wholesome* very clearly. I want them to hear it, know it, and use it. Being whole. Using all of one's self. A healthy mind and body. The interconnectedness of mind, body, and spirit. Now, perhaps, you are smiling and envisioning me as a male Pollyanna, but I will remind you that I consider myself a specialty act: Here today and gone tomorrow. I am not one of the "lifers" dedicated to helping these troubled youths on a daily basis. But since I believe in maximizing one's time allotment and maintaining an optimistic point of view, it became my goal to create just such a working environment, if only for ninety minutes of their day. I stress focus, cooperation, and mutual respect. Failing the lesson in cooperation is one of the reasons they've wound up here. They may be learning about movement and presence and body language, but they're also going to get the point that success can be obtained through cooperation and collaboration, whether on the basketball court or in the boardroom, by working together. I see their heads nod in comprehension. They can't deny the facts. OK! We are forming a community.

We begin standing in a circle. We are still. We quiet our bodies. Our goal is to look around the circle, connecting with the eyes of each participant. The eyes are important. They are where communication begins. These kids are not here for excelling in communication skills. Each session begins in this fashion. Quiet the errant energy to stillness and look into the eyes of your fellow "actor." The word excites them. I sense this. After all, what better to aspire to than a life like Eddie Murphy's? All that money! A great set of wheels! Until I find the opportunity to deem that goal as a far inferior one to creating a life that inspires and feeds them emotionally and spiritually, I let them have this one for a brief period: "How would you like to be spending your time while you're saving your first million?" And, as is common to any acting class, this leads us into sessions on emotions and the physicalization of these thoughts and feelings. I begin with the "thought" by putting it out there for them verbally and then requiring them to do nothing but *think* it. To see it in their mind's eye, visualizing themselves in a scenario in which they might be experiencing the specific emotion: anger, sadness, joy, confusion (and on and on). They are required to "build this scene" mentally, and as if watching a videotape of themselves, observe the movement of their bodies in action.

After this period of visualization, they are asked to find (exhibit) a position, stance, or gesture with their body that illustrates the specific emotion. They are asked to "arrive" at this stance at the count of three. I find this beginning and ending, joined by a three count, supremely effective in instilling a sense of physical and mental concentration and unity. It literally happens before one's eyes. They are concentrating mentally and physically. The next step is to familiarize themselves with that stance/posture, repeating it again and again in order to make it second nature. It's wonderful to observe these so-called communicationally challenged and often physically restless youths moving with care from stillness to an oftentimes revealing physical presence. Then we expand the posture/position by adding motion. Further exploration leads us to movement scenes. Eventually, we begin work on entrances and exits. I mark off a "stage" area with two chairs: one stage left, another stage right. One at a time, while the other participants observe, they do the "enter-deliver-exit" exercise, all without words. We let the body speak. We discuss entering with a purpose, choosing a spot onstage, "delivering the goods," and exiting with an intention. It is here that we also discuss an actor/character's past, present, and future. Where have I come from? What am I doing? Where am I going? The "delivery" time on stage is my way of describing what transpires there when communication and sharing occur. We discuss the scenes and guess at the details. I use this same exercise of thinking/feeling/imaging through posture to movement with the words *strong, free,* and *easy.* Thinking about these very positive words, imaging a personal interpretation, and then physicalizing it is a very informative experience for the teacher and an empowering one for the student. Afterward, simply reminding oneself of these words and the experience of them can prepare us to meet an upcoming challenge with confidence and security. In fact, I never give a performance that doesn't include this exercise in my warm-up and preparation. I tell them that acting is putting thought into action. So is life. You think about taking a sip of water. Then you pick up the glass and do it. It's an action. And action is movement motivated by desire, need, want. In these workshops, we spend ample time doing what I call "think and do" work. It's what an actor does. We think about the scene, the character, and then we put those thoughts into action by doing something. That "something" is not only motivated by the thought that preceded it but by our feelings about it.

I ask them, "What are you thinking? What are you doing?"

"I'm thinking about shooting baskets."

"OK, now do it. Great, great! Did you sink it?"

"Sure did!"

"Good. How'd you do it?"

"I saw myself doing it first."

Bingo. And later on: "What do you want to do out there in the world?"

"I wanna finish high school."

"Good, that's a good plan. Why do you want that?"

"I wanna make my mama proud. Get a good job."

"Terrific. Put that thought into action and follow the steps to see it through."

We discuss making positive choices. Wholesome choices. Wholesome thoughts to create wholesome actions. And while I'd like to believe that I am gentle with them, I do not believe that I am necessarily easy on them or that I am letting them off the hook. Acting is also reaction, making choices about how our character (we) will respond in a given situation, emotionally and physically, and then assuming responsibility (or not) for those actions. When someone insults me, do I smile and throw my hands into the air, or do I haul off and slug them? So, I ask these kids to answer this question for themselves. "How did you wind up in this place?" I tell them to look at the choices they made, imaging the action of the series of events that landed them here. Then I ask, "Do you want to come back?" Enough said! "Think before you act," I say. We're given this instrument of expression, our body. How can we best use it to our advantage and perhaps to the advantage of others? Will we make positive choices or negative ones? I say energize the wholesome ones.

Am I nuts? I'm asking these otherwise energetically off-the-wall kids to lie down and concentrate on their breathing as I guide them through conscious relaxation, talking them through their bodies while at the same time (unbeknownst to them) creating physical/kinetic awareness sensibility. I bring them to sitting slowly and then to standing. Then I teach each of them how to walk. Vertical. Lifting out of the pelvis. Confident. Strong. I'm laughing at myself here as I tell this; but we spend time carefully relearning that which we have taken for granted. I use the analogies of infancy and aging, observing through memory the care and caution with which babies learn to walk, learn to use their bodies; and the same care with which aging seniors must locomote through their days. We experiment with several types of walking and discuss the body language. We experiment with the energy of the voice. Once again, I use movement as a metaphor by describing the projection of sound through space as we "send" words, sentences, and phrases to one another across the room. I tell them this is acting. (Well, it is!) Again, they're surprised when I lead them into a discussion of similar parallels in life (i.e., Communication 101): Look directly at the person to whom you are speaking, and speak clearly in order to be heard and understood. They are not allowed to be shy in this group, though the embarrassed giggles are acceptable. Once we get into actual speaking and improvising dialogue, they are not allowed to say, "Know what I'm sayin'?" It is a rule! I tell them, "No, I don't! We don't. What are you saying? You tell us. Assume we don't, and explain it to us. Observe how you're using your body as you communicate your thoughts. And don't give me that communication cop-out sentence again! Thank you!" They get it.

What is occurring in these sessions is that which has occurred in every group of human beings in every imaginable situation since the beginning of time—the sense of community. And while all communities are not positively or holistically motivated, it merely illuminates the fact that this is what we do as humans. That it is a basic need: To belong, to find the place where we "fit," where we are unified and connected by some common sensibility, interest, or desire, whether it be our bowling team or our church group. We are a species that requires and values communication, and we do it first with our bodies through physical expression. In my workshops, we explore this through a series of exercises designed to become refamiliarized with our bodies; to listen to them, pay attention to them, and move with what I call the three Cs—commitment, concentration, and clarity—whether performing the simplest of tasks, such as resting our hand on our shoulder, or physicalizing a broad spectrum of characters that we reveal by engaging our imaginations. I also emphasize what I call the three Es. Now, the three Es are more advanced than the three Cs. You must pass through the Cs to get to the Es: efficient, effective, and effortless. Good words. Nothing negative there. Together it spells a mind, body, and spirit approach to personal empowerment in whatever scenario we imagine or actively create.

Driving home afterwards, I'm thinking about the terminology I'm using, the catch phrases I'm coining. And I ask myself, "When did you become such an old fart?" "Ah hell, it works," I answer aloud. You do what you do for an extended period of time and hopefully you realize, by paying attention, which of your catchy phrases get the desired results. If it works, use it.

Because of the specific needs of this particular population, I intentionally find a way to bring into each session how that which we've just done is reflected in the world "out there." How can we use this awareness to be effective out there? To make wholesome choices out there? To present ourselves in the best possible manner, communicating clearly and directly? I eventually lead us into a discussion of how we can utilize this information in applying for a job or going before the parole board or guidance counselor. At this time (remembering the importance of humor), I give myself permission to entertain them with my dazzling physical comedy and vocal mimicry, asking them if they'd hire me if I approached them like *this* (and I demonstrate): Slouched over, head hanging to the left of my chest, shuffling my feet, my pants pulled down to my butt, my hands jammed into my pockets, as I mumble some unintelligible something that is supposed to communicate the fact that I want a job. They laugh. I laugh. They get the point. Then we practice the "right" way. The one in the bible for excellent physical and verbal communication skills. It was always my hope and desire to make this experience bigger than an acting class. To provide some tools, create some awareness of self and of our responsibility to the human community.

I also include guided imagery in each session. While quietly relaxing, concentrating on breathing and awareness of the body, I talk them through a scenario (sometimes accompanied by music) in which they are to visualize an experience:

seeing and sensing their movements, colors, smells, sounds, and textures. In just such exercises, students have walked on the moon, felt the sun on their face, the sand under their feet, and on and on; including one youngster who went to heaven and touched his mother's hand. I learned afterwards that his mother had only recently passed away. In my workshop, by putting thought into action/movement, this young man physicalized that very personal and meaningful experience. I don't care whether they're cracking coconuts open with their teeth or saving the universe, as long as they're feeling something positive, and who knows, maybe even useful somewhere down the road.

Journaling is a most valuable tool that I employ in every session. After the participants have experienced the movement portion of the session, they are required to record what transpired in special notebooks. In these journals, they describe the scenario, its movement aspects, their emotional response to it, and any other personal observations. Generally, I read these in the evening, often being deeply moved by their insights, confirming once again that through movement of the body we are able to release and rediscover. I also incorporate various theater exercises too extensive to include here. I have always disliked the term *theater games*. Perhaps I should lighten up about this, but I don't like the childlike implications of that terminology. It smacks to me of that "performers are overgrown children" thing. That gets my goat! But that's another matter entirely and better left for conversations with folks who agree with me unequivocally.

I sincerely hope that the inclusion here of my attempts to make these workshops apropos to the real world have not come across as altruistic. But I cannot stress enough the positive results I have seen through carefully conducted movement workshops. And in situations such as these, it is my desire to provide an experience that may be lasting and impactive, something that these young people can take out into their world to use to their best and most wholesome advantage. And I hope my "specialty act" might give them something productive that will ultimately become their own.

Many of my extended workshops culminate in an informal presentation of the concepts and material covered during the sessions. I very quickly shape, guide, and direct the movement and verbal journeys we've collected. The audience usually consists of other residents, staff, social workers, and facilitators. It is remarkable to observe the transformation that has occurred as the kids put to use their new skills in presence, presentation, movement awareness, focus, and verbal expression—not the least of which is their acquired sense of pride. Pride in themselves, their participation, their group. They are a community.

Recently, I had an experience that once again confirmed for me the inesti-mable value of movement education and experience. I was to visit two classes in the theater department of a large and reputable university. I usually contact the professor beforehand to introduce myself and to discuss the topics currently being explored in the class in order that I might better suit their needs. It be-came clear in my conversations with the professors whose classes I would meet that they wanted me to speak about the creative process and about my process in particular. I confess that this is a topic that, like many actors, I enjoy run-ning on about endlessly. And while my procedure (and preference) is to pro-vide a movement/theater workshop, I allowed myself to be led into the discourse that seemed to be of specific interest to the respective professors. Never again! Though all went smoothly, I left with the feeling that I had not truly commu-nicated that which I am and that which I am about, my particular abilities and interests. In these two classes, I was just one more talking head flapping my jaw with theory and rhetoric. In the future, I will continue to have those previsit conversations, and then I will show up and proceed to do as I please. I will tell you why. I want these students to have an "experience." An actual physical experience that will evermore be cataloged in their mind/body/spirit memory bank. An experience that might in some way inform them immediately, at some unexpected time in the near or distant future, or in a manner in which they may not even be aware. It is for this reason that I call my course "Being (and Do-ing) in the Body." *Experience!* The advantages and consequences of an actual physical experience cannot be overestimated, for therein lies mystery.

Regardless of whoever we are and whatever we believe, we inhabit this won-derful instrument that we call the human body. Acknowledging the extraordi-nary potential for insight and enlightenment that it contains and accessing that power and information is truly being and doing in the body. Efficient, effec-tive, and effortless.

13
History and Development of the Halprin Life/Art Process

JAIME NISENBAUM

The Halprin Life/Art Process (HLAP) is a movement-based expressive arts therapeutic and educational approach taught at the Tamalpa Institute in Kentfield, California. This work, originated by dance pioneer Anna Halprin, is based on the interplay between the inherent knowledge of our life experience and its creative expression through the art mediums. This approach integrates movement, visual arts, performance techniques, and therapeutic practices to teach new models in art, health, psychology, and communication.

A significant part of the history of the HLAP is closely related to the life of Halprin and her unfolding relationship to dance. Over her now eighty years of dedicated and unstoppable exploration, this relationship has taken her from the exclusive ranks of dance as a performing art to the universal context of dance as a healing art. In this sense, her life's calling has brought dance back to its origins—to the larger community. Moreover, in the course of all these years, her career has broken long-standing conventions in dance and theater. Through her work, dance was redefined and became accessible and essential in many people's lives. Halprin challenged the ideas of the artist as a solitary hero figure and as an interpreter or commentator on life. Replacing these concepts, Halprin's work closed the gap between the lay individual and his or her creative expression by sanctioning the person's own life experience as the utmost kernel for artistic expression. This radical perspective whereby she reestablished the rich connection between life experience and art expression is one of the main tenets of the HLAP.

Many people from diverse fields such as psychology, education, architecture, and body-centered therapies, as well as dancers, actors, and musicians, have contributed both to Halprin's work and to the development of this approach.

Revised from a previously published essay in *Somatics Magazine* 11, no. 3 (fall–winter 1997–98) © 1997 by Jaime Nisenbaum.

Her radical performances and experimentations took place during the open and effervescent political, social, and cultural milieu of the 1960s and 1970s, which was informed by the provocative inquiries of the human potential movement. The cross-pollination between Eastern spiritual teachings and Western philosophy created an environment of influential people who began to create new models for personal growth. Among exponents of that era who significantly influenced Halprin's work are Moshe Feldenkrais *(Awareness Through Movement),* Ida Rolf (Structural Integration), Randolph Stone (Polarity Therapy), Fritz Perls (Gestalt therapy), Carl Rogers and Thomas Gordon (active listening techniques), and her husband and lifelong collaborator, Lawrence Halprin (environmental design and the RSVP Cycles).

In this section, I will describe some of the most significant events of Halprin's life and career in order to illuminate some of the elements that contributed to the development of the HLAP. For this purpose, I will divide her trajectory into four different periods, utilizing the progression of the life/art connection as our focal point. As we move along, it will become clear how Halprin's unwavering commitment to stay current with the events of her time and life has produced an outstanding body of work and has thus conferred on her the privileged position of a courageous innovator and seminal figure of our times.

EARLY BEGINNINGS

Anna Halprin began dancing when she was three years old. From her childhood until early adulthood, she was exposed to a wide array of classical and modern forms of dance representative of the 1920s and 1930s. This included the shoes and tutu of traditional ballet, Isadora Duncan's flowing veils, and the decorative oriental motif of the Denishawn school. In those years, dance as an art form was itself beginning its transition into a modern art, a fate already accomplished by painting, music, and literature.[1] Dance, especially in America, was looking for its own authenticity, a form that would give expression to a new aesthetic based on genuine human emotion. Rather than prescribed forms, modern dance sought to encourage movements coming from the impulses of the dancers themselves.

From 1938 to 1941, Halprin studied dance with Margaret H'Doubler at the University of Wisconsin in Madison, a connection that would deeply influence and inspire Halprin's later work. H'Doubler was an educator and biologist who "stressed personal creativity and the scientific study of anatomy and kinesiology over the values of dance as an art form in performances."[2] However, "caught up in the excitement" of the new forms of the great pioneers of modern dance in America (Martha Graham, Doris Humphrey, and Charles Weidman), Halprin "joined the ranks and for the next fifteen years was a modern dancer."[3] She moved to California with her husband, Lawrence, in 1945, and from 1948 until 1956, she taught and performed modern dance in a studio in San Francisco with dancer Welland Lathrop.

In 1955, Halprin participated as the only dancer from the West Coast in a dance festival in New York sponsored by the American National Theater Academy (ANTA). As she recalls this event, instead of finding the "freedom from form" purported by the modern dance movement, she "noticed that everybody in Martha Graham's company all looked like imitations of Martha Graham, everybody in Doris Humphrey's company all looked like imitations of Doris Humphrey. . . . I wasn't able to connect. I felt depressed, discouraged, distrustful and I knew my career as a modern dancer had just died."[4] This event, which marked Halprin's break with the modern dance establishment, catapulted her into her lifelong search for a dance that is primarily meaningful to the dancer, a dance that would join life and art.

Coming back from New York disillusioned with the preconceived and imposed styles of dance, Halprin left the Lathrop studio and moved to Marin County, where she developed her own work. There, in an outside deck located below her house, she began experimenting with new forms of dance in a workshop setting with some of her students who were interested in exploring and working together.

Halprin's search for authenticity in dance began with the exploration of the very roots of dance: movement and creativity. Instead of stylized form, she was seeking genuine expression. Drawing upon the repertoire of movement studies from her educational background with H'Doubler, Halprin initiated her research into the universal principles of movement (space, force, and time) and in its anatomical and kinesiological structures. As a result of these concentrated experiments with the physicality of movement, improvisations began to be infused with the individual's inner experience of the movement, thus allowing the dancers to bring their personal process into their dance. Subsequently, these improvisations evolved into interactions with other dancers within the group, and soon sound, voice, words, and dialogue began to be incorporated as part of the free-associative responses to movement.

Although her initial intention in this approach was to break away from learned and trained movement habits by fostering the dancer's own creative impulses, Halprin noticed that these improvisations were actually bringing the inner life of the dancer to the surface. In response to that, "we began to deal with ourselves as people, not dancers."[5] These workshops, which included dancers as well as musicians, educators, actors, writers, and therapists, eventually evolved into the San Francisco Dancers' Workshop (SFDW), which, fueled by the fecund and open experimental landscape of the 1960s, toured throughout the world, bringing innovation and controversy wherever it went. Halprin writes: "As we were deepening our life experiences we were simultaneously expanding our artistic expression. In the process of expanding our artistic expression we began to break down every known conventional dance and theater tradition."[6]

BREAKING THE BARRIERS BETWEEN LIFE AND ART

These initial performances by the SFDW were not always welcomed by the audiences. As a matter of fact, few were. Strong emotions and sometimes outrage and hostility would be stirred up as a result of the company's radical experimentation: People would walk out, talk loud, scream in the middle of the performances, and throw things on the stage or even at the performers.

These performances were the product of Halprin's research for a new dance. In this first period, among other explorations, she was looking for ways to eliminate the predictability of cause and effect. Everything that has to do with cause and effect, she said, would bring you back to habitual and "reactive" patterns. Breaking those patterns allowed for a more authentic dance expression in the moment, which was her ultimate goal. At the same time, she was also experimenting with utilizing spaces outside the proscenium and exploring the boundaries between performers and audience. Also characteristic of this period is a strong influence of existential thought. Her performances reflected an investigation of the real "heart" and meaning of a person's life. On the stage, the combination of all these elements was very unsettling. For instance, Halprin created pieces in which every element would be independent of the others. Music, movements, actions, and costumes were put forth in a very rich juxtaposition of sensorial input with no narrative connecting the events. What you saw was what you got. There was no meaning or grand scheme behind it; just like life. In *Five Legged Stool*, for example, staged in 1962, dancers used the stage, aisles, basement, and even the sidewalk outside the theater to perform mundane and repetitive activities for a whole two hours.

Another remarkable piece of this period was *Exposizione* (1963), performed in Italy, in which a huge cargo net was hung from the back of the theater diagonally down towards the bottom of the stage, creating the effect of a ramp that would start right from the orchestra pit. Performers would swing on ropes attached to the ceiling, wander between the seat rows, and carry automobile tires, bundles of rags and newspapers, and sacks stuffed with hundreds of tennis balls up the cargo net in a continual wave of repetitive activities, which were metaphors for the seemingly pointless cycles of one's life. The audience reacted violently by throwing things on the stage and talking loudly, and one man is said to have stomped down the aisles and in absolute rage screamed, "For this Columbus had to discover America!"[7]

The group, which now included, among others, dancers A. A. Leath, John Graham, Lynne Palmer, and Norma Leistiko and Halprin's two daughters, Daria and Rana, was emotionally affected by those reactions. At that time, Paul Baum, one of the participants of the SFDW, told Halprin about a psychologist who was doing some remarkable emotional work with people in San Francisco. Following that tip, Halprin and the SFDW began working with Fritz Perls, the founder of Gestalt therapy. Perls's work with the SFDW was tremendously influential in the development of the therapeutic applications of the HLAP. Moreover, his theater-like methods were instrumental not only in addressing the "charged" interpersonal relationships within the SFDW but also in deepening the relationship between art and life. Out of these sessions with Perls grew the possibility of further exploring the role of the audience in performances and utilizing its promising potential. Halprin realized that in expressing those negative reactions, people unconsciously also became performers. And because they were genuinely expressing themselves in the here and now, they epitomized what she was looking for: an authentic connection between life and art.

In this sense, those dissenting reactions opened the doors for the next period in Halprin's trajectory: to include the audience in meaningful experiences. This was facilitated by the other radical aspect of her work, for as the aisles, seats, and ceilings of theaters began to be occupied by the dancers of the SFDW, the walls separating audience and performer, life and art, began to come down.

BRIDGING THE GAP BETWEEN LIFE AND ART

As the barriers between life and art were being lifted, Halprin's work now sought forms to integrate dance and art into the daily life of the individual. Reflecting on her experiences in searching for her own dance, she knew that in order to achieve that goal she needed to create an art or a dance that would have personal meaning to the individual. She also knew that this meaning was found in the life experiences of the person. So, she began to close the gap between life and art by doing a radical experiment called *Apartment 6* (1965).

Originally, *Apartment 6* grew out of one idea: To utilize the complex relationship matrix that had been created between Halprin, Leath, and Graham over their fourteen years of working together as material for a performance piece. As Halprin explains, the rationale behind this piece was based on the fact that the performers in dance or drama are simultaneously themselves and their own instruments. There is no separation between the artist and the art medium as there is in visual arts or music. Therefore, the untapped psychological life of the performer in the here and now could be used as the material for a dance performance that would bridge art and life.

As Halprin admits, that was easier said than done. During a two-year preparation period, Halprin, Leath, and Graham worked under the supervision of a psychologist to clarify and work on their feelings towards each other. Then after that period, they brought themselves onto the stage. The program of *Apartment 6* read: "We'll listen to the radio, read newspapers, eat, talk. We may shout or argue, cajole or tease, or just sit quietly. The reality of doing, the reality of feeling, the reality of imagining. To play reality of whatever is happening. Because we are people, something will develop between us. The stage is where predetermined responses are no longer necessary. When the play is over, all will be forgiven and everyone will go home. Unless the play is life and life is the play."[8]

The response of the audience was mixed. Some didn't think that was dance and walked out. Others laughed and cried as they personally identified themselves with what was taking place on the stage. However, Halprin says, "It was not until the last, the sixteenth performance that I felt we had captivated what we wanted to do, which was to simply have two hours on the stage of a real-life situation, in which you as a performer and you as a person were completely the same thing. That finally happened. It worked for us and it worked for the audience."[9]

In *Apartment 6*, the audience witnessed persons performing themselves. Each person was his or her own art, and consequently the intermingling of art and life was immanent. Furthermore, those performances substantiated a philosophical principle that would have momentous significance in Halprin's work and therefore in the HLAP. In exposing themselves as real people on the stage, the performers were creating a new aesthetic: Beauty is what is authentic, or as Halprin put it, beauty "is the externalization of the now reality."[10] In this new aesthetic, beauty is the expression of the lived experience in the here and now rather than in form or technique. In the HLAP, the individual creates one's own style and becomes one's own art. This new aesthetic has been one of Halprin's most significant contributions to our times, and it is one of the underlying philosophical principles of the HLAP.

Championing her art and dance on the foregoing principle, Halprin began to explore her ideas with the public. This was the mid-1960s, and she applied that same aesthetic to the "happenings" of those times. In events designed for audience participation, she encouraged all kinds of people, especially nondancers, to participate in spontaneous performances on the streets, bus stops, parks, churches—anywhere but the conventional theater.[11]

Halprin's experiences with these happenings culminated in a series of different audience participation events called *Myths* (1967–68), which she did in collaboration with Patrick Hickey. In spite of the clear participatory purpose stated in the announcements for these events, people came to *Myths* expecting a performance. But instead they found themselves performing.[12] Basing each evening on universal themes like sexuality, aggression, conflict, atonement, or celebration, Halprin involved the audience in rituals through which the participants could release their own creative impulses. The results were sometimes chaotic, other times ecstatic. Nonetheless, one way or the other, these experiments were bringing ordinary individuals closer to their creative expressions.

As Halprin reflected on those events, she came to a realization that would eventually expand her artistic mission and transform her relationship to art and dance: "I am coming to see the artist in another light. She is no longer a solitary hero figure, but rather a guide who works to evoke the art within us all."[13] Halprin then began working more and more towards disseminating her vision of the life/art connection into the wider social and political sphere. One of the first examples of this new broadened path was *Ceremony of Us* (1969), a performance that came in response to a social and political crisis.

After seeing the involvement of the audience-performers in *Myths,* James Woods, the director of Studio Watts in Los Angeles, invited Halprin to hold a workshop for African American artists shortly after the race riots in Detroit and Watts. Woods was interested in using Halprin's work in his "at risk" community. As she considered that invitation, Halprin proposed that she would run simultaneous and parallel workshops for a whole year, one for blacks at Studio Watts and one for whites at SFDW. After that year of working separately, the two groups would come together and work towards a joint performance.

Ten days before the performance at the Mark Taper Forum in Los Angeles, the two groups came together for the first time, and the spontaneous interaction between blacks and whites became the material for *Ceremony of Us.* As it was Halprin's trademark, the audience was also invited to participate in a way that would allow them to encounter and experience their own racial issues. So as the audience entered the auditorium, they had to choose to come in either with the all-white group or with the all-black group. At the close of the performance, seeing the resolution that happened on stage between those two groups, the audience formed a procession that resulted in a spontaneous dance of performers and audience members, blacks and whites.

This yearlong experience with *Ceremony of Us* inspired Halprin to form a multiracial dance company with Asians, Chicanos, Latinos, and Native Americans. As Otter observes, "Each artistic experience opened new avenues of exploration for Anna. . . . She saw that by applying dance to various groups of people, themes would emerge out of the needs of the participants, which would serve to bring them together. And particularly, the process of dance that she was developing showed promising signs of healing the wounds that existed between groups with differing value systems and life styles."[14]

However, with the excitement of working with such a varied group of people came also the challenges. Halprin and the group became painfully aware of the diversity of those "value systems and life styles" that also manifested themselves in staggering differences in movement characteristics. A new system of communication was urgently needed for the group to work together. This system needed to support that diversity of perspectives and weave that patchwork of experiences together into a common quilt. Halprin found this new method in the RSVP Cycles, a system for collective creativity that her husband had developed. In short, the RSVP Cycles provide a map that makes the creative process visible and thus encourages group participation and involvement. Today, the RSVP Cycles are an integral and essential part of the HLAP. Within this system, there lies the tools that support individuals, as well as groups, to engage in a creative process that fosters both personal and artistic growth.[15]

The work with this multiracial group evolved into a dance performance called *Initiations and Transformations* (1971), which toured the East Coast. Although the performance had a basic structure, which is called "score" in the HLAP, each presentation was different. The score not only invited personal expression in the moment but also allowed each presentation to respond to the different environments in which it was performed.

As a result of this approach to her work and performances where personal expression is encouraged, Halprin began to come across universal themes that cut below the racial, economic, social, and cultural differences between people. By tapping into the life experience of each person as the source for creative expression, she realized that there were common themes that ran through the lives of every person and would eventually surface in their creative enactment in dances and performances. She then started to investigate the archetypal character of the dances people were creating and discovered that those dances had transformative powers. The dances transformed the dancers because they were meaningful to those who were performing. So, she began to call her dances *rituals* and the material that generated them *myths*. In her own words, Halprin explains: "The reason I call [the performances] myths and rituals is because we are telling our own stories that define our life. When we express those stories creatively and artistically I believe we touch a universality, and we have a chance to see ourselves as parts of a larger humanity. And this in turn becomes a powerful force for deep transformation within the life of a person as well as an entire community."[16]

The life-size self-portraits and other drawn images that participants would create during her workshops were also an invaluable resources for Halprin's research into the aforementioned archetypal themes. For instance, she noticed that water, trees, snakes, birds, knives, and walls were symbols that revealed themselves in the participants' drawings in almost every workshop. The recurrence of these images suggested they had an archetypal significance that was beyond the personal life experience of the individual. However, rather than attach a preconceived meaning to any of these images, she allowed the participants to "discover" their meaning and purpose in their lives. One of the techniques utilized for that discovery was the Psychokinetic Visualization Process, which is an intrinsic component of the HLAP today. Participants would "dance" or enact their self-portraits and other drawn images, utilizing spontaneous responses evoked by the images. From these enactments, life themes based on the individual's life experiences would arise. The collection of those life themes formed what is called the individual's "personal mythology," which would then be utilized as material for performances called "personal rituals."

In this journey from the personal to the archetypal, Halprin found the path that would take her relationship to dance to an even wider social scope: the use of dance to facilitate the healing of personal and community issues.

DISSEMINATING THE LIFE/ART CONNECTION:
DANCE AS A HEALING ART

This fourth period of Halprin's trajectory is characterized by the extending and weaving of those personal myths and rituals into the larger symbols, archetypes, and myths of each community. This consequential step in her career grew also out of a life-changing personal experience.

In 1972, Halprin drew a self-portrait that she was unable to dance. It contained a black ball near her pelvic area. Intrigued by her own resistance to express that symbol in her movement, she made an appointment with a doctor. He diagnosed cancer in her colon, precisely where she had drawn that black ball. She went through the traditional surgical procedures, and the cancer was removed. Three years after that surgery, she had a recurrence. However, this time she was determined to confront her cancer through her own art.

Over a period of several months, she drew a series of self-portraits that she then enacted in performances witnessed by family, friends, and students. Reflecting on this process during which her cancer eventually went into spontaneous remission, Halprin noticed a pattern that "seemed relevant to other healing processes."[17] This map, which she called "The Five Stages of Healing," consisted first of *identifying* the issue. The second step was *confronting* the issue (in her case, the self-portrait enactments), which was then followed by a *release*. The fourth stage was *integrating* the changes in her body, and the last step was *assimilation,* "a coming back to my community and my family and my life."[18] Later on, the Five Stages of Healing were further developed by Daria Halprin into a more comprehensive system that not only maps the healing process but also offers a blueprint for personal growth. This system, which is called "The Five Part Process," is one of the central components of the HLAP.[19]

After that experience with cancer, Anna Halprin began to dedicate her dance to promote healing of both personal and community issues. From this new trajectory of her career, there is one seminal event that holds special relevance, for from its seeds would eventually evolve an annual global ritual for peace and healing of the Earth called "Planetary Dance."

In 1981, Anna and her husband offered a nine-month workshop called "The Search for Myth and Ritual through Dance in the Environment." The intention of this workshop was to discover a living myth for that particular community of people who were gathering and working together for those nine months. At that time, Halprin recounts, "There was a trailside killer who'd been on Mt. Tamalpais and killed seven women on the trails over the course of two years, and so the trails were closed, and this became a spiritual issue, because the mountain was closed to [all of] us. I felt that the issue there was violence in our society, and the attack of our spiritual dimension, because the mountain is the spiritual symbol of our landscape."[20]

As images of Mt. Tamalpais began to appear more and more in the drawings during the workshop, it became clear to all the participants that the living myth that they were searching for was being enacted "right on their backyard": the violence on the mountain. So, through a series of events, which included performances by the group on the top of the mountain, tree plantings, poetry readings, and a final collective performance, this workshop raised the awareness of the public to the issue, and the whole local community became involved in the process of reclaiming the mountain. A few days after that last performance, the killer was caught following a tip that came from within the community.

This community ritual, originally called "In and On the Mountain," evolved over the years into "Circle the Earth," as Halprin began utilizing the same basic structure of that ritual to confront other community issues such as homelessness, AIDS, cancer, child abuse, environmental destruction, and racism. As Rachel Kaplan puts it, Circle the Earth "has been the physical manifestation of Halprin's search for a dance that has a use and function in contemporary culture and consolidates not only her earlier quest for total theater, but her research into collective creativity, community, illness, and recovery."[21]

The Planetary Dance evolved from Circle the Earth as the myths enacted by a specific community began to offer a window into even larger issues of humankind. As Halprin points out, in AIDS, racism, sexual abuse, or environmental destruction, for example, lie the mythological polarities between life and death, ignorance and consciousness, men and women, self and other. As a result of this movement towards encompassing the larger issues of our lives on Earth, the Planetary Dance has transformed itself into a peace dance that is performed in thirty-six countries around the world on Easter, Earth Day, and the spring equinox. Halprin's vision for the Planetary Dance is one of a collective ritual that will be performed by people around the globe, "an intentional action which generates its own end: peace and peaceful coexistence."[22] These are the ultimate goals of the life/art connection and of dance as a healing art.

THE HALPRIN LIFE/ART PROCESS TODAY

In 1978, the Tamalpa Institute was cofounded by Anna and Daria Halprin to promote the life/art connection, to foster the uses of dance as a healing art, and to provide a context for training programs on the HLAP. As the radical experimental phase of the 1960s and the mid-1970s was coming to a close, Daria Halprin began synthesizing the artistic aspects of the HLAP with its intrinsic therapeutic elements. Her goal was to promote the marriage of art and science and to articulate the "technology of the work" so that it could be further developed and taught to others. Talking about this process, she says, "What I have found particularly meaningful is the emergence of theory out of lived experience over the past twenty years—my own, my clients', and my students'. I am more and more convinced that there is a need to continue to develop and articulate a body of theory which communicates what we have and are discovering about art as a healing force."[23]

Daria Halprin's book *Coming Alive* reflects this effort and provides both the theoretical and practical frameworks for the applications of the HLAP in the field of expressive arts therapy and education. "Basic to this approach," she says, "is the perspective that the physical body is completely interconnected with the thinking and feeling realms of the individual; that an integrated life includes and honors the integrated creative expression of all these levels of our human experience."[24]

Today, the Tamalpa Institute offers training programs and classes for individuals who wish to incorporate the principles and tools of creative expression into their own professional practices and personal development. Graduates of the institute work in a wide variety of settings, including corporations, hospitals, mental health organizations, schools, and artistic communities.

CONCLUSION

As she contemplates her lifework, Anna Halprin sees that there is one thread that has been an ongoing aspect of her journey: "an attempt to find a process that unites personal and artistic growth, life and art, with one aspect continuously feeding off the other and coming together in new ways."[25] In an interview with the *Village Voice* back in 1975, she had described her journey thus far: "You know, you start opening one door, and there's another door. And you open that one and there's another one. I just kept going into as many doors as seem to be in front of me. And I haven't found the end."[26] To those of us familiar with her work and the HLAP, as we look back at these past decades since that interview, it seems that she is still opening new doors for herself and, consequently, for all of us who are inheriting the legacy of a body of work so impressive in its scope and in its significance to our times.

NOTES

1. Howard Gardner, *Creative Minds* (New York: Basic Books, 1993), 266.
2. Anna Halprin, *Moving Toward Life: Five Decades of Transformative Dance*, ed. Rachel Kaplan (Middleton, CT: Wesleyan University Press, 1995), 3.

3. Anna Halprin, *Discovering Dance* (Kentfield, CA: Tamalpa Institute, 1982).

4. A. Halprin, *Discovering Dance.*

5. A. Halprin, *Moving Toward Life,* 79.

6. A. Halprin, *Discovering Dance.*

7. A. Halprin, *Discovering Dance.*

8. Roger J. Pierce, "The Anna Halprin Story," *Village Voice* (1975): 4, quoted in *Anna Halprin's Second Collected Writings* (San Francisco Dancer's Workshop, 1975).

9. A. Halprin, *Moving Toward Life,* 99.

10. Quoted in Pierce, "The Anna Halprin Story," 10.

11. Ken Otter, *My Search For a Living Myth* (Santa Monica, CA: University Without Walls, 1984), 12.

12. A. Halprin, *Moving Toward Life,* 130.

13. A. Halprin, *Moving Toward Life,* 131.

14. Otter, *My Search,* 13.

15. For more information on the RSVP Cycles, see A. Halprin, *Moving Toward Life,* 124–25; and Lawrence Halprin, *The R.S.V.P. Cycles* (New York: George Brazilier, 1969).

16. A. Halprin, *Discovering Dance.*

17. A. Halprin, *Moving Toward Life,* 67.

18. A. Halprin, *Moving Toward Life,* 67.

19. Daria Halprin, *Coming Alive* (Kentfield, CA: Tamalpa Institute, 1989).

20. A. Halprin, *Moving Toward Life,* 20.

21. A. Halprin, *Moving Toward Life,* 186.

22. A. Halprin, *Moving Toward Life,* 186.

23. Daria Halprin, *Art and Movement as a Healing Force.* (Kentfield, CA: Tamalpa Institute, 1996).

24. D. Halprin, *Art and Movement.*

25. A. Halprin, *Moving Toward Life,* 111.

26. Pierce, "The Anna Halprin Story," 10.

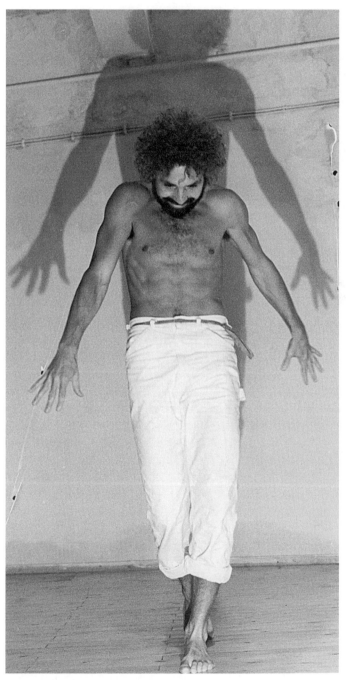

G. Hoffman Soto, an instructor at the Tamalpa Institute, in his own solo dance. Photograph printed with permission from G. Hoffman Soto.

Dorothy M. Vislocky *(facing camera)*, a professor emerita at Hunter College, teaching a class. Photograph by Nat Tileston; printed with permission from Dorothy M. Vislocky.

Shirley Ririe, codirector of the Ririe-Woodbury Dance Company and a professor emerita of the University of Utah, in her own solo dance. Photograph by Mark Wagner; printed with permission from Shirley Ririe.

Michael Hoeye *(facing camera)* and other former Washington University dance students in their own group composition. Photograph by Washington University Photographic Service.

Carol North, the artistic director *(foreground)*, and other members of the Metro Theater Company in *Mud Weavings,* a theater piece by Zaro Weil. Photograph by Morton D. May; printed with permission from Carol North.

Branislav Tomich, a former student at Washington University, in *I Recall,* a suite for three chairs and solo performers, choreographed by Annelise Mertz. Photograph by Richard N. Levine, Washington University Photographic Service; printed with permission from Branislav Tomich.

A former Washington University dance student in her own compositional study titled "Suspension." Photograph by Tom Stewart, Washington University Photographic Service.

A Washington University student performing her own compositional study for children. Photograph by Washington University Photographic Service.

"Spring Celebration," an improvised ritual, led by Anna Halprin, cofounder and artistic director of the Tamalpa Institute. Photograph printed with permission from Jeff Rehg.

Students of Jeff Rehg in "Spring Celebration." Photograph printed with permission from Jeff Rehg.

A Washington University student performing her own compositional study for children. Photograph by Washington University Photographic Service.

"Spring Celebration," an improvised ritual, led by Anna Halprin, cofounder and artistic director of the Tamalpa Institute. Photograph printed with permission from Jeff Rehg.

Students of Jeff Rehg in "Spring Celebration." Photograph printed with permission from Jeff Rehg.

Claudia Holzapfel, a former dance major at Washington University, in "Youkali," choreographed by Annelise Mertz. Photograph by Washington University Photographic Service; printed with permission from Claudia Holzapfel.

Murray Louis teaching a master class at Washington University. Photograph by Gail Cissna, Washington University Photographic Service; printed with permission from Murray Louis.

Dance for children composed and performed by a Washington University student, with a prop designed by Margot Clark. Photograph by Washington University Photographic Service.

Sue Gash, a former dance major at Washington University, and Satoru Shimazaki, a former artist in residence at Washington University, performing "Duet for One Voice," choreographed by Annelise Mertz. Photograph by Bibi Stromberg; printed with permission from Bonnie Jacobson and Sue Gash.

"Minuet for a Structure" performed by a former dance major at Washington University, choreographed by Annelise Mertz. Photograph by Herb Weitman, Washington University Photographic Service.

Gale Ormiston, a former senior artist in residence at Washington University, in the solo piece "Vortex," choreographed by Ormiston. Photograph by Washington University Photographic Service; printed with permission from Gale Ormiston.

14

Spring Celebration: A Movement Ritual for Children

JEFF REHG

"Spring Celebration" evolved from Anna Halprin's movement piece "Planetary Dance." It is an annual event for children five to twelve years of age and an opportunity for the children to connect to their world in their own special way. The event has a flavor of its own—not as a set event but rather as a concept—because the individuals participating create the event itself. Because of the flexibility and openness of its subject matter, the ritual incurs few limits on the depth of its meaning for participants.

WHAT IS THE CELEBRATION ABOUT?

Spring is a time for new life coming forth. This celebration is a time to focus on how we are connected to other things beyond ourselves, especially to elements of the natural world—plants, soil, water, and air. Participants will find a new source of energy within themselves to enhance their connections to this world.

PRIOR TO THE DAY OF THE EVENT

As the ritual leader, you should meet the children and talk with them about circles: Are there circular patterns to their lives? Can they see the pattern of the seasons, the school year, the moon, the cycle of the sun and of the rain, plants and animals being born, living, and then dying? This is a celebration that uses circles. The celebration's rhythm should be provided by one or more large drums.

Practice rehearsal. The leader should stage a practice rehearsal prior to the celebration:

entering the celebration
sitting in the circle

101

getting up one at a time
calling out their intention
running outside of the four directions
following the rhythm of the drums
stopping, lying on one's back, and being still

The four directions. Explain the directions that will make up the circle and how each direction has its own special meaning and magical powers. Be sure to ask participants to wear colors for the celebration that represent their direction: North will honor the strength and beauty of the Earth. If a child chooses north, he or she should wear green. East will honor the wind and air, which symbolizes wisdom and learning. East's color is yellow. South will honor fire, which symbolizes warmth, compassion, and love. The color of the south is red. West will honor water, which symbolizes relaxation and renewal. The color of the west is blue.

The run. Each participant should decide what they will run for or what they feel connected to. As they run, each footstep placed on the Earth will strengthen that relationship.

The chant. Teach a chant to be sung while entering the celebration. Give the children permission to improvise in their singing with the guidance of the Great Spirit.

the earth, the wind, the fire, the rain
      return, return, return, return
the earth, the wind, the fire, the rain
      return, return, return, return

hey-hey, hey-hey, hey-hey, hey-hey
      ho-ho, ho-ho, ho-ho, ho-ho
hey-hey, hey-hey, hey-hey, hey-hey
      ho-ho, ho-ho, ho-ho, ho-ho

ON THE DAY OF THE EVENT
(WHAT MAKES UP THE CELEBRATION?)

The children should enter the park (or meadow, whichever is used) quietly and in a focused manner, chanting. Forming the entire circle, they should settle in the direction that they have decided to represent. Have the ritual leader call in the four directions, giving thanks for everyone's being part of the circle together. The children should stand up one at a time, call out, "I am running for _____," take a pinch of grass seed, and throw it to the earth. Then they should turn to the outside of the circle and begin to run in a clockwise direction. Let this continue until all the children are up and running. Drums should keep the beat.

Children can stop and rest at any one of the four directions and then run again, rest, and so on. As the energy begins to wear down, speed up the drums, increasing the pace. Get everyone back on their feet and running, faster, faster, faster. And then *boom!* the drums should stop all at once. Have the children drop to the earth wherever they are. Lying on their backs, with their hands over their hearts, everyone must be still and quiet, paying attention to the earth touching their bodies, the wind entering with each breath, the fire of their hearts pounding, and the water and moisture inside them.

While the children are lying still on their backs, looking out into the universe, and paying attention to the energy of life, give them time to just lay there in silence. Then the leader should have the children gather all their wishes, prayers, and good thoughts into their hands. At the count of three—one, two, three—*pow!* they should throw their hands into the sky, releasing their wishes. As they begin slowing, have them sit up. Snacks may then be served, bringing the celebration to a close.

The leader should begin the *sharing*. While the children are eating their snacks, encourage individuals to talk about their experience during the run and the thoughts they had while lying on their backs.

Supporting activities. On the day of the celebration, a number of activities can extend and enhance the meaning of the day's event, such as face painting and craft construction (headbands, shakers, streamers, or wands).

Breakdown of tasks. The following responsibilities will need to be fulfilled to stage the celebration:

Ritual leader—organizes the event: rehearsal, explanation of the event, chanting, and general sequence of events

Starters—get children to stand up, to call out what it is they are running for, and to start running

Keeper of the circle—guides children to run on the outside of the circle, not cut through the middle, and keeps children from wandering off

Parent greeters—approach parents as they arrive at the event and welcome them to the celebration

Circle runners—participate in the run itself, keeping all the children moving in
the same direction, directing children that stop to sit and rest at one of the
four directions, and helping any children who fall down
Snacks coordinator—distributes snacks to the four directions at the end of the
celebration

I invite you to be a part of this circle, to open yourself to this experience, open
your eyes, your ears, your minds, and your hearts to see the magic that is present.
As you journey around this circle, you will have questions from both within
and from without. You may discover something about yourself: Who you are,
what you already knew, and what is possible for you during this lifetime.

If humanity is to grow, then we must all have a better understanding of this
circle that you are always traveling around—even when you rest. Each of you
will enter at a different point, and your entrance gives you certain powers, gifts,
and responsibilities that no one else will have nor truly understand. Yet, as you
pass others different from yourself, you have the opportunity to learn, and from
this learning you can keep your own life force beating within your heart.

In this vision, I see a way to teach, an opportunity for people to change, to
grow, to be open to life, to be open and aware of their relationship and their
responsibility to life while here on earth. I also see that this vision is a vision for
today—for tomorrow will bring with it new and different thoughts. It is a vision that is capable of providing a place for healing with new beginnings. While
our bodies are in motion, our minds and hearts will be full and open for growth.

The essence of this *dance* is movement, allowing yourself to experience whatever is presented to you as you travel the circle. Learning may come to you as
a thought, an animal, a rock, or a plant or just from listening to the wind, yet
allowing yourself to be mindful and present during this time.

If we dance with our hearts open, the light of love and unity that created
the universe is then able to shine in. As we start to travel and run this magic
circle, our hearts will naturally begin to pound and to open wider as we learn
to experience life and accept that we have all been given a task to perform our
part in life, with all of its beauty and challenges.

Claim your sense of self and your intention in life as you enter and begin
to *dance*.

15
Teaching Dance to Children

ANNA HALPRIN

I began to teach dance to children in 1940 as a student intern at the University of Wisconsin where I was getting my undergraduate degree. In Boston (1942–43), I taught children again, both at a settlement house for impoverished youth and at a private school for children from wealthy families. I learned an important lesson during those years about the environmental influences on movement, socialization, and childhood development. When I moved to Marin County, I became instrumental in developing the Marin County Dance Co-operatives (1947), and through the dance co-ops, I taught dance for the next twenty-five years to children in the community where I lived. I loved teaching children, and I learned many things about creativity and spontaneity from children, which later found their way into my work as a performer and teacher of other artists. The following text is excerpted from my writings of 1949–57.

THE MARIN COUNTY DANCE CO-OPERATIVES

The Marin County Dance Co-operatives were a collective enterprise, fueled by the energy of the parents, children, and all the communities involved. The mothers assumed the responsibility of management. Together, they designed exhibits and posters and planned special events to keep the whole community informed of the activities of the dance cooperatives. The purpose of the dance co-ops was to give Bay Area children and adults an experience in creative dance and an awareness of the potential of rhythm and movement as they are manifest in daily life. The co-operatives were an entirely independent organization functioning under the management and supervision of community members. The Dancers' Workshop faculty provided qualified instruction and assured the maintenance of the highest possible educational standards, but it was the

Revised from Anna Halprin, "The Marin County Dance Cooperatives: Teaching Dance to Children," from *Moving Toward Life* © 1995 by Wesleyan University Press, by permission of the University Press of New England.

voluntary participation of the parents and friends that made these classes possible at a minimum cost and well within the means of the average family group.
(Classes cost fifty cents apiece. Teachers for the co-ops were trained at the Dancers'
Workshop and included A. A. Leath, Norma Leistiko, John Graham, and many
others.) There were fifteen dance co-ops functioning in various communities
in the area, and it has been estimated that these co-ops provided direct opportunities for dance training to more than two thousand people each year.

The Marin County Dance Co-operatives were a fascinating and successful
example of the organic development of dance within the life of a modern community. To my knowledge, these co-operatives constituted a unique experiment
in the United States. After three years, they had grown in size, number, and general community acceptance. Every indication exists that they fulfilled a real need
in the life of this California community. We believe the story of the Marin
County Dance Co-operatives is applicable to other communities and other areas of life.

The immediate stimulus for beginning the co-operatives was a children's
demonstration of dance that I coordinated. Some Marin County parents were
present and pounced on the idea of dance classes with great enthusiasm. They
decided at once that Marin should have dance classes of that sort and determined to organize the classes themselves. Meetings were called by the parents,
and almost overnight, a space was allocated for classes, which started naturally
enough with the little girls. Soon there were demands for boys' classes, and the
mothers bought themselves leotards. Classes grew and grew, and the co-operatives became more active. Soon dance concerts and demonstrations were sponsored, and dance literature was made available to the community. The moving
force behind the whole organization was the hardworking mothers who, having organized the classes, collected tuition, checked on attendance, and arranged
for classrooms, kept the co-operatives functioning. They not only kept the
classes active and alive but made the whole idea an important element in the
life of the community. Through them, dance extended its influence throughout
the whole fabric of Marin County.

What is the significance of the Marin County Dance Co-operatives? First,
they are symbolic of the possibility of reestablishing a community's direct participation in an art form. Second, the dance artist and teacher was given the dignity
of place within his or her own community. Third, because of the nonprofit element of the co-operative, large numbers of people could afford dance classes.
This would, it was hoped, raise the level of excellence in the dance product.

Probably the most exciting aspect of this experiment was to see art fuse with the life of a community, to watch its influence on children and adults, and to see it grow from something alien and esoteric to something very alive and close and fun to be a part of—a truly cooperative, communal enterprise.

THE ROLE OF THE TEACHER

It is important that the child's everyday experience be brought into focus by the teacher in the dance class. It is also an enhancement that the teacher adds to whatever is lacking in the child's realm of experience. The teacher can bring this approach to class by knowing the characteristics of the child's age level, being aware of his or her background influences and keeping up with the subjects he or she is learning in school. The teacher must also have established a friendly and sympathetic atmosphere in the classroom so that the children are free to respond. From the response of the children, the teacher can get a cue whether to dance about fairies and flowers, or fire engines and scribbly houses, or just a wiggly movement with a sudden stop. In teaching this way, you never know exactly what will happen in advance of a class. The teacher must plan, but the plans need to be flexible. Therefore, a children's class is never repeated the same way twice. Each class should be a creation in itself—a complete dance drama that captures the essence of a child's life in that one moment.

DANCE EDUCATION AND TRAINING

We can think of training, first of all, in terms of a learning process. For children to learn and to progress in technical training, they must have a desire and interest in this direction. What enthusiastic students they will become if they are aware not only of "what" they are doing but "why" they are doing it. If their technical training is grounded in a kinesthetic awareness of movement, it will be a pleasurable experience. If, in the presentation of a movement idea, the teacher permits the students to take an active role in its development, and they are given the freedom to try for themselves until the movement "feels right," they will be able to find meaning in what they are doing.

Children like to be engaged in the "process" of learning. They need to be encouraged to have input in what they are doing. Their dancing will then have personal meaning, and their attitude will be alert, passionate, and enthusiastic. Over a period of time, they develop initiative and self-discipline. They find zest and joy in the learning process. They must be continually activated in their learning in order to develop. A wise teacher will give increasing demands and challenges with a very careful respect to the children's level of development, thereby avoiding discouragement and frustration by not forcing the children beyond their capacity. The children, when ready to meet these new demands, can then work with concentration for the desired control and refinement. Their achievement of these ideals will give them the motivation to continue.

In addition to the process of learning, there is a question—"*What* are they learning?" They are learning the science of body movement itself, rhythmic factors, elements of force and space, and the relationships of moving with other people, among other things. They are also learning how to discover dance ideas from what they feel, see, and hear. They learn how to use the materials of dance to shape movement experiences into patterns and to create forms for their dance ideas. The result is that their knowledge is not limited to rigid techniques but rather to fundamental materials of dance that draw upon the vast potential resources of the children themselves and the principles of art.

A technical training of this nature will enable the children to acquire aesthetic values of images of beauty that emerge out of their own wellspring of responses. What one child has created is shared with others in the class, what they have created as a group is shared together, and in this way, the children gain from each other a breadth of aesthetic values. Because each child has formed his or her expression in his or her own way, there are individual differences. Seeing these differences helps all the children be flexible and open-minded, appreciative and responsive to the feelings and attitudes of others.

A training that integrates technique with expression at every level of the child's growth will bring forth a child who dances with spontaneity, the freshness and vitality of the expressive mind flowing through the muscles and nerves. When children are trained in the disciplines of intrinsic art principles, they dance with great grace and freedom.

16
On Teachers

MURRAY LOUIS

My teaching career began at the Henry Street Playhouse when *they* decided that the afternoon hours were to be filled with children's classes. When *they* decided that the income was necessary. When *they* decided that the long tradition of children's classes should be continued. When *they* decided that I should teach them. I was led into a room filled with children, the door was closed behind me, and my teaching career began.

The next fifteen years were years of love. I took hundreds of kids through their childhood and adolescence. Professionalism, or a career in dance, never entered my vocabulary. These kids were brought to dance as a living experience, yet they worked with a stronger dedication than many adult professionals I have taught. Dance meant something to them. It wasn't just steps. Of course, they believed in me, they trusted me, and that belief was one of the greatest responsibilities I have ever faced in my career. Although I have since stopped teaching children, I always remember with great affection my years with them.

I would arrive Saturday morning for a 9 A.M. class, sore and exhausted after a Friday night performance. There they were, expectantly awaiting me with days of accumulated exuberance. I fed them, and they supped. After five hours, they left, and drained and exhausted, I could turn my thoughts ahead to the evening's performance.

I remember one day in class when things had gotten out of hand. My patience was stretched, my nerves taut. I had lost control of the energy I had stimulated. I stood in the center of the room and grimly waited to grab the first kid who passed me and show that class that I meant business. My reasoning had sunk to that level. When I felt someone close behind me, I turned. A little seven-year-old figure, waist high, came closer and leaned against me. I hovered over my victim. Then she looked up and said, "I'm standing close to you," and I melted. It was then that I understood that the profession had its rewards. The child was not being sentimental, but in the midst of my chaos, she had made a simple statement of order. Teaching became for me a way of practicing order, or as Alwin Nikolais says, sanity.

The rewards of a career in the arts aren't exactly going to win first place at Dun & Bradstreet nor rate a bronze bust, but fulfillment of some sort is expected. In this profession, dancers have the direct satisfaction of the doing, choreographers have the satisfaction of realizing their choreography, but teachers must wait to see the results of their giving. Sometimes they must wait years for this reward. Sometimes it seems a lifetime. Dancers and choreographers pace their careers with short-term investments, with performances and opening nights. Teachers have longer commitments and tend to see the forest, not the bouquets. Commitment is a very difficult idea to define.

I teach because I want to know more about my art. I suppose in a way I'm a scientist. I question and answer. I dissect principles to get at their pulsing hearts. I drive my classes until I've split the molecular structure of a given movement phrase. I experiment, I distill, I clarify, and I keep out of the way of my discoveries. Dance has its own identity, and I teach it objectively. But being objective is not easy. Teaching can be a very subjective business.

Dealing with students is a constant tempest. How do teachers ever get reconciled to the inevitable exodus of their best students? Even admitting that that's the name of the game, it is still heartrending each time a favorite or a talent leaves. What can a teacher say when a third-year student, after taking one class elsewhere, breathlessly announces a major breakthrough? How does a teacher face kids who have worked diligently and hard to tell them they just might not make it? How much does a teacher interfere with talents who are ruining their lives with screwed-up heads? When does a teacher cry "halt!" to students who glibly take what they have been taught and teach it as their own elsewhere?

Experience prepares teachers to teach. It is only through teaching that one learns to teach. It is only through teaching that one knows what one knows and learns how to present and articulate it. Preparing for the profession doesn't necessarily begin with a teacher-training course. I had a professor during my college years whose offensiveness was so thorough it could only be protected by his tenure. He turned off just about everyone taking his classes. I realized then that if I taught kids, I sure as hell knew what I wouldn't do, and that was to turn kids off.

What draws teachers to this profession, aside from earning a livelihood, is the inherent understanding of the important role they play in keeping the art together and the accepted realization that they have been chosen to play that role. Everyone in the profession goes through the classroom. The classroom allows everyone the chance to achieve his or her own identity. Hopes, dreams, and ambitions are all played out there. Only dance—the nonverbal language of the art—is spoken there. There is no need for apologies, just achievement. And at the helm of it all is the teacher.

The teacher stands at the crossroad of the dancer's world: One rein on the creative, one rein on the technical, one rein on the aesthetics, one rein on the living process, one rein on the future, one on the past, all of them straining at the same time. With the skill of a Roman charioteer, one maneuvers this thundering energy towards some goal. The Muses pause to watch. Another flight has been made; another class has been taught.

17
Dance

EMMA D. SHEEHY

Movement is the infant's first instinctive reaction to life. The infant is not consciously aware of it but, except during sleep, is getting constant experience in its use. In addition to automatic reflex movements that give pleasure and satisfaction, the infant soon begins to learn a measure of control over certain movements in order to achieve a goal. Is there anything more delightful for the observer than the experience of watching the infant's beginning explorations as it struggles to get a finger in its mouth—feels around in space and, finally, satisfactorily resolves a need?

EXPLORING MOVEMENT

Do we ever stop to think of the skill that is required for the toddler to balance on two feet, maintain equilibrium, and walk? The acquirement of a similar feat of physical coordination is rarely equaled by the average adult in later life. Rolling and crawling, pushing and pulling, running and jumping, children are showing us constantly their delight and their "at-homeness" in movement; climbing and exploring, with leaps and bounds, they are all over the place.

"To prevent bodily weakness and infirmity, exercise is necessary: and one physician has said that he did not know what was most necessary to the human frame, *food* or *motion*." Over one hundred and fifty years have passed since this statement appeared in *Youthful Recreation,* a magazine published in Philadelphia. It would be interesting to know what this physician meant by *motion.* Was he thinking of some prescribed form of exercise, of games, of dance, or of the usual normal activity of daily life? The demands of our early farm and village life went a long way toward satisfying the needs of physical development that in present-day life have to be artificially provided for. Whether or not our forebears were conscious of the importance of motion, it was of necessity a part of their very existence. It is unlikely that they were psychologically aware of the therapeutic and physical values inherent in the movements necessary to carry on day-by-day living, but youth got on with "exercise" just the same!

If we watch any group of four-, five-, or six-year-olds, we shall find that a large part of their time is spent on the floor, either in such activities as block building or just in the sheer physical enjoyment of tumbling around. Boys and girls of elementary-school age find other ways of exploring movement since adults are not usually sympathetic to older children's engaging in the kind of activity deemed acceptable in the younger child. Older children soon learn that tumbling and other similar uses of the floor are not what is expected of them, and they reserve their antics for times when adults are not around. But youngsters are resourceful, and even in the most formal schoolroom, they find ways and means of moving of which even they are unaware.

Have you ever really *seen* the many inventive and ingenious ways a boy has of getting out of his seat? Have you *seen* the ways he uses his legs and his torso while he is sitting, even when he is deeply interested in his work? Have you *seen* what movement happens when excited and eager children raise their hands to reply to a question? Not long ago, after a college class in which we were trying to awaken and extend our perceptions in movement, an experienced teacher of ten- and eleven-year-old children saw for the first time the ways in which the children in her class raised their hands. Here are a few of her observations: "holding arm straight out on a diagonal and sharply jiggling it back and forth; increasing the range by making their arms turn in a full circle about their heads; changing direction and level as they half stood up and rapidly changed the arm they were raising, at the same time there was a shift of body weight; changing focus and direction by crossing their arms in back of them and more or less hugging their heads; decreasing the range as arms were held taut and wrists were shaken." This teacher's observations made all of us *see* in a way we had never seen before and encouraged us to bring new eyes to the movements in day-by-day living with children.

How much more interesting to pick up papers around the wastebasket by squatting and hopping around the area than in the way a grown-up would do it! Stairs are a chore to the adult; to the child, they offer adventure—two steps at a time, backwards, sideways, eyes closed, reaching the top or bottom by two steps forward and one step backward. Two-and-a-half-year-old Johnny reached the bottom of the stairs ahead of his teacher, then stopped, and jumped from the second step. Teacher's heart skipped a beat, and then she stood at the bottom and encouraged him to do it again. Over and over, he jumped and then learned to walk backwards up the lower steps. He had conquered the world.

Children are constantly talking to us in movement. They are showing us what is important to them; they talk with their hands, their heads, their eyes, their legs, their bodies. All of this is related to dance, for the basic elements of dance are movement and rhythm. John Dewey reminds us that the aesthetic arts are the "enhancements of the processes of every day life."[1] It is from living itself that the great dancers and the choreographers draw their material. In a news interview, Clark Jones, who directed the telecast of the *Cinderella* ballet, commented on the unique possibilities of choreography for television, for example, choreography for fingers and eyes combined into the whole fabric of a composition. What would a Clark Jones see in a class where children were waving their hands in reply to a teacher's question? Perhaps not a dance composition, but he would surely see possibilities of which our dim eyes and kinesthetic perceptions are unaware.

Let us look at five-year-old Tom on his way to school as he goes the distance of a long block, weaving himself scallop-fashion from one side of the sidewalk to the other, so as to touch the hood of each car parked along the curb. For Tom, walking that block each morning is an adventure in the exploration of space and a growing awareness of the possibilities of space. Tom and countless other Toms and Marys are, *appropriate to their stage of development,* dealing with a very important aspect of dance—space—the increased awareness of it and its possibilities being one of the major contributions of Mary Wigman to the dance.

Children are not dancers in the sense that years of study, devotion, insight, and training make the professional dancer, but they are constantly dealing with the stuff of which dance is made—movement and rhythm. They are unaware of what they do, they transcend the know-how and do the impossible because they will to do it. Professional dancers, aware of what they do and how they do it, can control and recapture a movement to express what they wish to communicate.

A moving child, moving in a nonconformist way, can be a threat to a grown-up in school. We are afraid of what might happen, and so we tend to discourage movement experimentation except through regular channels, such as games and the use of equipment. At the same time, we talk a great deal about creative dance and rack our brains to motivate a group of youngsters to use movement creatively at dance time! Classroom teachers reach out for techniques, questions to ask, dramatic ideas to interpret, and music that will evoke movement, hoping that the children will respond. Many of the children do, after a fashion, but there are usually one or two for whom this is sissy stuff. Yet, these same youngsters, during free time, show remarkable skill in the way in which they use movement. But they do not know that these natural impulses to movement are the raw material of dance, and usually we do not know it, either. It takes the kinesthetic sensitivity of a dancer, a dance choreographer, or a dance photographer to see the roots of dance in these basic movements.

CREATIVE RHYTHMS

But there is more to dance. We hear a great deal about "creative rhythms." Nursery schools, kindergartens, and elementary grades have creative-rhythm programs. Music is played and children are urged to interpret it. There is a question, however, of how much real creativity is possible when music is the sole stimulus of dance.

Perhaps if we compare the art of movement with another art, painting, for example, we can see more clearly how we have unintentionally handicapped children in their use of movement as it relates to dance. When we give paints to children, we do not tell them what to paint; we encourage them to use their own initiative in experimenting with color and line. Their first interest is in the art material itself and what they can do with it, and the teacher will not hurry this stage.

In movement, however, we play music for children and ask them to listen to it and "do what it says"! In other words, we start out with a framework into which we expect the children to fit their ideas. If we were to carry this method over into painting, we should say to children: "Here are paints that you may use in painting a picture of a house." But someone will say: "Yes, we play music, but we tell the children to do what they like to it." Carrying this analogy further, we should then say to the children who are painting: "You may paint any kind of house you wish, but you *must* paint a house!"

When music is played for children and they are asked to move to it, a pattern and a mood are set that limit the type of movement. Or we have the situation in which music is played, but the children do whatever they please, regardless of the accompaniment. In the first case, a child's creativeness is limited; in the second, music ceases to have any meaning as related to the movement.

Programs are built around animal rhythms, mechanical rhythms, transportation rhythms, and so on. Each set of rhythms has its own particular music, played either on records or on the piano. Depending on the way in which the teacher works with boys and girls, a certain amount of invention and ingenuity may be encouraged. Dramatic ideas stimulate the use of the entire body in a way that is not possible with folk and square dancing. The sensitive teacher, working together with a group of children, can release imagination and make it possible for desirable skills to be developed. But what the child does must be appropriate to the music. Not a few teachers, however, have gone beyond the bounds of the limitations of music and are working freely with children in the field of movement exploration itself. Even if one is not a dancer, a study of what movement means in modern dance can give one a truly exciting insight into the possibilities of dance with children. Gladys Andrews suggests many techniques intended to make both the teacher and the children more aware of the possibilities of the great variety of body movements.[2] The emphasis is first on movement itself and second on the interpretation of music.

MODERN DANCE

A consideration of the more liberal interpretation of creative rhythms leads us directly into an examination of "modern" dance and what its underlying philosophy has to offer those of us who work with boys and girls in the elementary school.

One of the greatest contributions made by modern dance has been its recognition of the independence of movement as an art medium. Music is used to support movement; it is part of the scenery; it is the handmaiden of the dance. Many times it is composed especially for the dance, since music that will clearly interpret the movement cannot always be found. Those of us who work with children have much to learn from a study of modern dance if we are to be understanding guides of their use of movement. We have given children the opportunity for unhampered physical activity on the playground during their free periods; but as soon as a small group comes together for dancing, we have been too eager not only to tie their ideas immediately to music but also to use music as a stimulus. We forget that children's ideas and their urge to sheer physical activity are a much more powerful and vital stimulus than any music we can offer and a far more rewarding one if we wish to capture their enthusiasm. We must therefore give them every opportunity to use their material, the material of movement, and train ourselves in recognizing their natural functional movements as our most important asset in teaching. Their movements spring from feelings and needs that are strong within them. The expression of these in movement has vitality, and if we give it encouragement and support, its own unique form evolves.

It was her quest for the essence of dance that led Isadora Duncan to reject the prevailing dance forms of her day. Dance had become so crystallized and surrounded with so many sterile techniques that she could not find herself within its framework. She turned to the dances of the early Greeks not because she wanted to dance as they did but because she wanted to find out why they danced as they did. Duncan was responsible for the birth of what has come to be known as modern dance.

Mary Wigman, who has been credited with freeing dance from the domination of music, was also in search of the essence of dance.[3] Her idea for a dance sprang from within her, and she had the courage to allow this idea to find its own form without any preconceived pattern.

Great dancers such as Duncan and Wigman threw aside the thwarting tendencies of tradition and recognized that the artistic vitality of their contribution lay in the development of techniques peculiar and unique to the individuals and to the ideas they were creating. Should this knowledge not give us courage as we work with boys and girls? We are not trying to train professional dancers in our schools. We say over and over again that we want our children to have the joys and satisfactions that attend dance, and then, by our insistence on stressing *first* even the simple techniques of leaping, skipping, and keeping time to music, we unintentionally put obstacles in the way.

Take, for example, the concern of both adults and children when a child is a "one-footed" skipper. Such approaches as teaching children to hop first on one foot and then on the other focus attention on technique, and they become self-conscious and more removed than ever from the goal. Skipping has to do with the feeling of lift in the body, reaching to the sky. If the adult focuses on this and takes the children by the hand, skipping with them and taking attention away from their feet, it isn't long before they become "two-footed" skippers. From the standpoint of the children, are we not trying to help them capture the "why" of skipping, just as Duncan tried to find out why Greek dancers danced as they did?

Think of all of the other movements in which the one-footed skipper may be skilled, types of movements involving the entire body that are used so much by modern dance. But we do not recognize them in a skipping, jumping, and marching program as being part of dance, and so undue emphasis is given to these few techniques. Many a dance teacher believes that children cannot begin to create until they have learned and mastered these skills. The teacher may see no dance possibilities in the countless skilled uses of the body, floor movements of all kinds, the twistings and turnings and wigglings and squirmings (if you wish), the almost impossible (to adults) stunts and tricks, the ability to crawl into an idea and project the feelings that inspire it. These are skills that, to a degree, even nursery-school children have and that, unfortunately, they too often learn are not respected even in kindergarten, because we want them to express themselves in our particular brand of movement.

For too long, we have identified the means to the end with the goal. This has been pointed out to us innumerable times by such great thinkers as Alfred North Whitehead and Albert Einstein. We take on and give precedence to the techniques of an art rather than assiduously cultivating the essence of the art. The movement of modern dance exemplified this search for meanings, and that is why, I believe, a study of it as conceived by the great dancers in the field holds so much for us in our work with children. In recent years, it has lost its creative vitality, in some instances, through preoccupation with "systems" or "schools" of technique.

Writing on dance as a means of communication, John Martin, former dance critic of the *New York Times,* gives us a clear and direct definition of modern dance:

Indubitably no other art form has been so inaptly named as the "modern dance." Not only is the phrase non-descriptive, but it is markedly inaccurate, since there is absolutely nothing modern about modern dance. It is, as a matter of fact, virtually basic dance, the oldest of all dance forms. The modern dancer, instead of employing the cumulative resources of academic tradition, cuts through directly to the source of all dancing. He utilizes the principle that every emotional state tends to express itself in movement, and that the movements thus created spontaneously, though they are not representational, reflect accurately in each case the character of the particular emotional state. Because of the inherent contagion of bodily movement, which makes the onlooker feel sympathetically in his own musculature the exertions he sees in somebody else's musculature, the dancer is able to convey through movement the most intangible emotional experience. This is the prime purpose of the modern dance; it is not interested in spectacle, but in the communication of emotional experiences—intuitive perceptions, elusive truths—which cannot be communicated in reasoned terms or reduced to mere statement of fact.[4]

This principle is at least as old as humanity itself; primitive societies, as we have seen, have found it so potent that they have called it magic and based religious and social practices on it. But it had never been consciously utilized as the basis of art, so far as any record exists, until the turn of the last century, when Isadora Duncan made it the very center and source of her practices, and the so-called modern dance was born.

In his lectures and writing, Martin has pointed out two forces hostile to the development of modern dance (we shall continue to call it *modern dance,* because the name is used so generally; but we hope the reader will keep in mind Martin's concept of *basic dance*): first, the domination of music, and second, the literary mind. The thoughtful consideration of these two obstacles and the relegation of both to their appropriate places in the art of dance should give us a deeper understanding of movement as a creative medium in itself. A constantly growing increase in our knowledge of the scope and variety of movement, *attended especially* by a developing kinesthetic sensitivity to it, will promote this understanding. Some of the obstacles that get in our way and keep us from accepting and working with the movements that have deep meaning for children will be identified as we go along.

INCREASING OUR UNDERSTANDING OF DANCE

We cannot teach something we do not know. We can, however, be *knowing* about that something—in this case, movement—in a way that will help us live with children so that we recognize and *see* with understanding eyes and feelings the dispositions and skills they already have. The following are a few of the ways in which we can learn more about dance and children.

Observing Children and Its Implications

Teachers have long been encouraged to observe children to obtain a better understanding of how they grow and develop. The mental, emotional, social, and physical aspects of development have been the focus of observations. While movement and rhythm are not unrelated to these, for the purpose of studying dance we shall focus directly on the movements of children. Our best laboratory here is found where the children are unsupervised: their free play on the streets, in the playground, and in the backyard; the ways in which they go about their chores in school; their movements when they are quiet, while reading, watching television, or listening; and the countless other situations in which they are unaware of their movements or when they are consciously practicing skills in doing stunts.

What is happening when a seven-year-old boy walks backwards and zigzags up the stairs with his eyes closed? If he has been sent on an errand, this may not be the time for "movement loitering," for it may take *three minutes* longer than if he dashed up the steps. We shall have to decide if the saving of three minutes is a matter of greater importance than his experience both movement-wise and in relation to relaxation. Can we be "tolerant of trances" as "he feeds on time"?[5] Is it *time* that annoys us or the fact that he is using the stairs in an unconventional, though not antisocial, way?

To the imaginative child, and certainly to the dancer, the use of space is an adventure. The most interesting distance to a point is not a straight line! Have you ever watched the ways in which dancers use even a very limited space—the space possibilities they feel, horizontally and vertically, in the development of their dance ideas?

Can we allow for and utilize children's talent for space in our dance programs? Can we say to them, "This is what you do, and you do it well, so we shall do more of it"? Can you recall the glow that you experienced when someone approved something you had been doing, and how you bent every effort to do it better? Living with children in such a way offers the kind of soil for learning that cannot possibly be achieved with artificial motivation.

Let us put the idea of exploration of space to work in a typical school "rhythm" session where the group marches together. Usually, the goal is keeping time to music. Once that has been achieved, the "march idea," with one or two possible variations such as tiptoe marching, has been exhausted! Children are trained to go in one direction, the teacher believing this necessary so that they will not bump into each other. The nonconformist youngster who starts to walk backwards, to weave in and out, or to go in the opposite direction is promptly reminded that this isn't the way to march. The child either conforms or stays on the sidelines. The muscular impulse that the child had toward variation and toward making a monotonous movement interesting is not recognized as a lead to a more advanced level of marching and certainly a more artistic one.

Why? Simply because we assume that children cannot walk in varying directions in a group without getting in each other's way. *But they can,* as the teacher of fours, of eights, and of twelves well knows who has encouraged this kind of exploration. "Find out as many different ways of marching as you can— *as long as you do not interfere with anyone else.*" Anyone who does not respect this can be removed from the group, and rarely will this happen more than once. For this is fun, this is adventure, and well worth accepting the restriction. As individual children in the group begin to explore space in interesting ways, the teacher can call attention to them one at a time, and everyone can try these variations out. In other words, there are thirty possible teachers in a group rather than just one.

From Hannah Klein, a student teacher who saw and accepted a child's way of hopping around the wastebasket while picking up bits of paper, comes the following thoughtful understanding of her own increased awareness of children in the classroom.

In watching children as they move about the room working, unaware that they are being observed, I have been amazed at the variety and complexity of the movements involved. It is impossible to discuss the free movement of the children without also discussing my change of attitude which has accompanied these observations. In the example of the child picking up the papers, my first impulse was to tell him to pick up the papers as quickly as possible without hopping around. However, I stopped myself in time. What difference did it make if it took a few extra seconds to pick up the papers?

I have found that the most interesting times to watch the children's movements are during the transition periods. After snack time we have a short session in which we clean up, turn one table on top of a second, and stack them against the wall. My cooperating teacher and I turn the tables on top of each other, and two children push the tables to the wall. It is while they are waiting for the teachers to come and turn tables that all kinds of interesting movements take place. The table is often used in the same capacity as the bar in a ballet studio. Arms and legs go flying; bodies are twirling, bending and stretching. Here too, I have put the reins on myself. I once saw a boy doing some kind of arabesque with a beat (making the calves of his legs meet in midair) and was about to come out with some "schoolteacherish" comment to the effect of, "Is that the way to help?" when I caught myself just in time. It isn't that long ago that I stood at a bar in dancing school while the ballet master *laboriously tried to get us to master* just that step!

Children often approach me with new and interesting movements which they have thought up at home or have noticed themselves doing! They know that I am interested. I have also tried to tie in movement with other things we are learning. We are trying to develop the concept of roundness. We have a science tray of things that roll and through experimentation have discovered that round things roll but square or straight things don't. Recently I read the children the story, *A Kiss Is Round*. We then found parts of ourselves that were round and things in the room that were round. Now I tried to fit in movement. "Can you make yourself round?" Immediately I had a group of round little balls on the floor. At my suggestion they were soon demonstrating the things they could do if they were round. We all tried the individual stunts of the various children, rolling, turning, rocking, and rolling just one leg or arm to mention a few. We stood up to see how we could go around while standing. "Did we have to stand still to go round?" "No!" They showed me how they could run *around* the room, skip *around* the room. We got into a circle and went around together. By this time everyone had had a grand time, had exercised his muscles, had used his body actively and creatively, and had increased his concept of round.

"They know that I am interested." This is the key with which this teacher is able to unlock the door for her children and for herself—in this case, the door to dance for five-year-olds.

Vicarious Experiences

Movement in and of itself has a peculiar fascination for most of us. The incoming waves, the wind in the trees, rocking in a chair, watching the turntable of a record player, the revolving ferris wheel and carousel, horses racing, cars passing, and countless other similar experiences can contribute to our relaxation and sense of well-being if we allow ourselves to "tune in" with motion.

Sitting quietly in a seat at a dance concert can be a vital and tingling experience if we identify kinesthetically with the dancer. Many come away from seeing *Oklahoma!, Carousel,* or *The King and I,* either the film or a stage production, with a heightened awareness of movement, and for those who live closely with children, there is a quick realization of the similarities between the physical stunts and antics of youngsters in their unsupervised play and many of the body movements of the dancers. Children *are not* miniature dancers—dancers have an acute awareness of every part of their body and call upon it at will to communicate their dance. But the freshness in the sure, pure use of the body that the child has captivates the attention of the observer who is movement-minded.

Mime is another art medium that can cultivate a greater sensitivity to movement. The very isolation of movement in this art makes for a greater impact on the observer. Do the gestures and the almost imperceptible movements of children take on new meaning for us as our eyes have been opened to wider movement through the enjoyment of mime? I especially recommend the films of the French mime Marcel Marceau, such as *In the Park.*

Dance has come into our homes today on the television screen. Theatrical productions, religious programs, and even commercials call upon many forms of dance to convey their messages. I wonder if we are aware of the many ways movement itself is used by advertisers on television to accent their sales arguments! Turn down the speaker and watch. As a matter of fact, it is sometimes interesting to look at dance without sound.

How much do our children learn about movement from television? There is a feast of movement available for them, but we cannot possibly measure it, nor are we always aware of the meaning they take from any particular program. A mother recently reported that her two young children were fascinated with wrestling matches. After observing one herself, she saw no reason why this should prove to be so attractive until she discovered them zealously practicing the movements used by the wrestlers without any interest in wrestling with each other. A thoughtful study of dance on television and the movie screen and in photographs of dancers can contribute greatly to our knowledge of dance. One's movement sense cannot help but be quickened by the beautiful and artistic film *The Works of Calder,* distributed by the Museum of Modern Art in New York. In this film, viewers have a rare treat in color and motion as they watch the mobiles of Alexander Calder and movements in nature. The music accompaniment is by John Cage, in twelve-tone style, consisting of harp and Chinese gong for the most part. (The longer, uncut edition of the film is recommended.) What a fascinating adventure can be ours as we read about dance in such autobiographies as those of Pavlova and Duncan and in the numerous books on dance written for the lay person.

Direct Experience in Dance

There is no substitute for personal experience in dance. Fortunately, most teachers have had some experience in one or more forms of recreational dancing. A few have studied modern dance in high school or college, but it is the exceptional teacher who is a trained dancer.

Personal experience in modern dance can be a tremendous asset in working with children. If we have not had it, one is never too old to go in search of it, *provided* the right teacher is secured. My own first four tries in modern dance classes proved to be not only exhausting but altogether concerned with technique, the premise being that once the techniques were learned, I could start to dance. Since my intention was not to become a dancer but rather to become familiar with what is considered to be the essence of dance, I very soon decided that these classes did not meet my need nor could I keep up with them! Perhaps fifteen or twenty years earlier, they would have been more appropriate. I was fortunate, however, in finding a dancer who was interested in what I outlined to her as my needs, both for myself and for teaching children. She was one of those rare teachers who was able to identify with her pupil rather than teach a preconceived system. She, too, was interested in children not as a "trainer" but as a learner. She visited my group a number of times and opened new horizons to me because of the significant movements she saw in children's spontaneous play.

I have known several classroom teachers trained in modern dance who were able to teach their students a few of the lesser techniques of dance but whose focus was so technique-oriented that they saw no possibilities in children's spontaneous movements. Were they afraid of children? Did they not respect the use of their bodies, and did they not see skills in such use? Or was their way of living with children so limited that there was little opportunity for any kind of movement?

On the other hand, not long ago I observed a physically handicapped teacher so alive to the possibilities of dance in her class and so able to release her students' movement potentialities that an observer might have thought this class had been taught by a skilled dance teacher.

Skill in, and knowledge of, modern dance can be a rewarding experience for classroom teachers, providing they are able to cut through to the heart of dance rather than concern themselves with the techniques. Not that techniques are not important—as children consciously and avidly practice a trick or stunt, they are using a technique, one that evolves directly out of the situation and has real meaning for them.

Our most important job in teaching dance to children is with ourselves. The foregoing discussion has been directed toward the encouragement of a constantly growing recognition of the vocabulary of movement. The more we see and feel for ourselves, the more we see in children. The philosopher Martin Buber reminds us of this power of awareness: "Nothing can be done without awareness. With it, anything is possible." The conscious pursuit of awareness in dance and the recognition of the many faces of dance are rewarding not only in teaching children but primarily in one's own growth. And it is in the minutiae of daily living where we can discover so much, as a student recently expressed so well: "While walking along the street, I have tried to think of, for instance, how my big toe *feels* at that particular moment or to watch my hands doing various activities. A sensible amount of this mind training will, I think, help me in seeing more in children." Barbara Mettler's picture book of creative dance is especially helpful in developing awareness.

We can cultivate a consciousness of movement in its myriad forms—how people walk, how they sit down, how they use their hands, their shoulders, and their eyebrows, and how their bodies respond to the countless stimuli in daily living. The great dancer is aware of all of these and many more. We shall not be dancers in this sense, but at least we can enjoy a deepening understanding of the meaning of dance.

NOTES

1. John Dewey, *Art as Experience* (New York: Putnam, 1934), 6.

2. Gladys Andrews, *Creative Rhythmic Movement for Children* (Englewood Cliffs, NJ: Prentice-Hall, 1954).

3. Mary Wigman, "Composition in Pure Movement," *Modern Dance,* Jan.–Feb. 1946. Reprinted in *The Creative Process,* ed. Brewster Ghiselin (New York: New American Library, 1955).

4. John Martin, *The Dance* (New York: Tudor, 1963), 105.

5. From the poem "Boy Dressing" by Mark Van Doren.

18
Up, Down, Round, and Round: From Creative Dance to Dance Therapy (A Personal Retrospective)

JOANNA G. HARRIS

At the University of Wisconsin in 1953, I, along with other members of the Orchesis Group, was asked to dance for inmates of prisons and hospitals. We performed informal dance events at such facilities. When we were confronted by the staff at Mendota State Hospital, we were asked, "Why don't you dance with them [the patients] instead of for them?" After much consideration and review of our own skills, we responded. "Yes, we'll begin with the children." We had been trained to work with children.

Dance therapy, as practiced in the last five decades, began with children's creative dance, and most group sessions still use its methodology: a simple, personalized warm-up, basic skill development and self-assessment, improvisation, individualized attention, closure, relaxation, group acknowledgement, conversation. We go up and down, round and round, and still the validity of creative dance sustains the work.

Marian Chace is considered the "mother" of dance therapy in the United States. In her writings, she tells us that she "frequently spoke to parent-teacher groups at their request on the value of continuing the participation of children in dance as an important aspect of living in their development and growth."[1] Chace had been a dancer with the Denishawn Company. Settling in Washington, D.C., when her performing career ended, she opened a studio and taught adults' and children's classes. Some children in these classes had parents who were involved with the National Institute of Mental Health, specifically St. Elizabeth's Hospital. Her work in Washington became recognized; she was asked to train elementary school teachers and to hold sessions in orphanages and at the National Training School for Girls. All this was preparation for what she would develop as dance therapy, though in the early years at St. Elizabeth's Hospital, it was called "dance as communication."

My own work began in the classes of the Duncan Dance Guild in New York City. Fifty years later, I learn that Duncan Dance is taught and performed in studios from San Francisco to Prague and from Moscow to New York. The end of the nineteenth century was a revolutionary time when many basic premises were examined, including the nature of childhood. Duncan, in her studios in France and Russia and with her sister Elizabeth in Germany, brought the possibility of expressive activity to children as well as a new freedom with their bodies. Are we much further along at the beginning of the twenty-first century? We acknowledge the need, but do we provide the opportunities? Some progress has been made, but all over America children grow up with little or no movement education.

I started teaching children when I was fourteen. I learned well how to choreograph the circle dances, adapt the floor work, and structure the improvisations that brought both pleasure and discipline to young people. I understood the organization of music, at least the classical works we used in the Duncan Dance. Those disciplines continue to structure my work as a dance therapist. When I did undergraduate work at the University of Wisconsin with Margaret H'Doubler, my skills in teaching dance were strengthened. I acquired the necessary knowledge underlying the biology and kinesiology of dance. I was ready to adapt dance skills for the challenged child.

My first opportunity came while I was earning my master's degree at Mills College, in Oakland, California. As part of a research project, I volunteered to work with the autistic children at Langely-Porter Neuropsychiatric Institute, the psychiatric teaching hospital of the University of California, San Francisco. There was little or no psychoactive medication in those days; the children wore straitjackets and lived in rooms with bars on the windows. Their range of activity was limited and erratic. They often hit themselves with hands or knees, injuring eyes and ears. It was a sorry, sad situation; everyone thought I was a bit mad myself to believe that these children, ages four to eleven, could participate in dance activities. But we took the straitjackets off, held their hands, and eventually they danced—and sang.[2]

As I settled into the San Francisco Bay Area, as an instructor at UC Berkeley, I continued the work at Langely-Porter, trained others in the basic theory and practice of dance therapy, and moved my work to the Napa State Hospital. The psychiatric model soon changed; schizophrenogenic mothers were no longer being blamed for their children's condition. The cause for autism was

considered to be vitamin deficiency, then it was insufficient early socialization, then it was brain damage followed by in utero genetic malformation. We
still don't know. There was a new theory and a new treatment every year.
The children moved from Langely-Porter to Napa State Hospital and into adult
training programs. The symptoms remained: rocking back and forth, toe-
walking, twirling, lack of eye contact, perseveration, mutism. I brought more
and more students with me to establish one-to-one contact. We were still
dancing and singing. Sometimes, it was the only recreation that both the staff
and the patients shared. But they did share it, and for a short hour, some nor-
malcy prevailed.

No one was ever cured. Sometimes, rapport was established. Often, skills were
learned and retained. But we did create an energetic environment in which lots
happened. The staff got braver. Everyone had a sense of humor about themselves
and the work. And best of all, most of the children stayed with us for a full half
hour! For these patients, we considered that a real achievement: socialization
through dance, some participation, and a few instances of motivated movement.

I continued this work during a teaching stint in Pittsburgh, Pennsylvania.
Groups of autistic children used the facilities of a local synagogue school for
an afternoon program. The temple was near the Carnegie Institute of Technology, where I was teaching in the drama department. By this time, the middle
1960s, there was more sophistication in patient assessment though not yet many
breakthroughs in treatment. I was able to work with individual children in a
more focused setting. I held them; we rocked, played finger games, repeated
rhymes, clapped rhythms, and hopefully retraced some of the developmental
motor stages that had gone unfinished. It was good work.

In the years following, as I developed graduate programs in Creative Arts
Therapy in several West Coast colleges (at Lone Mountain, at Antioch, and
through the University of California extension), I was able to establish intern-
ships in dance therapy for children's in-patient wards and out-patient services.
Some of these are still maintained, though the mental health system in California does not support many in-patient institutions. In 1979, as a Fulbright fellow in Great Britain, I was able to do an extensive study of treatment programs
for children in schools and hospitals. There the support patterns are more extensive. I was able to coach teachers, nurses, and psychiatric staff in the fundamentals of dance therapy and helped to extend the already established work
with varying populations, including children with physical handicaps as well
as emotional problems. The basic teaching and intervention patterns are the
same nationally and internationally: slow repetition of basic skills, adaptation

of essential motor patterns to creative play, the use of imagery, music, props, and language, physical stamina, and thorough observation skills. These take at least ten years to develop, but they serve a lifetime.

For many years, the American Dance Therapy Association (ADTA) did not honor the work being done in schools as dance therapy. The clinical model begun in St. Elizabeth's Hospital was too strong. In time, the changes in school programs and the need to expand children's services changed all that. The ADTA just celebrated its thirty-third anniversary. Many practitioners of dance/movement therapy made the transition to the therapist's role from teachers of dance and creative movement. As we expand our knowledge and understanding of the therapeutic role dance plays in children's lives, we are able to extend this work to children in many settings. The last five decades present a dramatic unfolding of that work. Let me document some selected programs.

One of the pioneers of dance therapy with children is Jane Manning. Her work in Los Angeles began in the nursery schools of that city and continued in the studio she shared with Mary Whitehouse and later at the Cedars Sinai Hospital and other child guidance clinics. Her model is developmental; she says, "The whole mastery of movement . . . is not only crucial to the physical development of the child, but to the feeling the child has for himself, for herself . . . if one can get back to that place where the exploration of movement was so important . . . it has a healing effect."[3] Other dance therapists, whose work is discussed in *Dance and Other Expressive Art Therapies*[4] are Judith Pines Fried, Steve Harvey, Bette Blau, Tina Erfer, Susan Loman, and Diane Duggan. In an earlier volume, *Dance/Movement Therapy, A Healing Art,* Fran Levy cites the work of Blanche Evan, Elaine Siegel, Beth Kalish Weiss, Marcia Leventhal, Elizabeth Polk, and Jane Downes. Levy speaks of their work:

> In summary, those who work with learning disabled children emphasize using body movement in a structured and organized fashion as a tool for conceptual learning and body image development. The dance therapist's active participation, verbal and non-verbal, as a structuring agent and educational guide, is paramount.
>
> . . . We must add the approach of Jane Downes. Downes sees freedom of expression as a basic tool for the healthy development of full selfhood. The goals of her treatment model are to enable the children to become aware of their own resources, to perceive themselves as worthy beings, to communicate ideas and emotions, and to experience their own senses as an active force in their lives.[5]

In England, it is important to note the work of Bonnie Meekums, whose special practice has been with mothers and children working together. Marian North of the Laban Center was certainly the British pioneer of dance therapy. Other British dance therapists of note are Helen Payne, Kedzie Penfield, Kristina Stanton, Monika Steiner, and Sarah Holden-Williamson. The work of most of these practitioners has been detailed in *Dance Movement Therapy: Theory and Practice.*[6] Very good and very extensive work is also being done in Israel, particularly by Judith Mendelsohn at Hebrew Hospital in Jerusalem.

Current attention in the field centers on the areas of family therapy, child abuse (from adults and other children), and adolescent problems from delinquency to anorexia. A poignant plea for attention to children who abuse one another was made at a recent dance therapy conference by SuEllen Fried. In a recent book, *Bullies and Victims,*[7] Fried identifies seven "prevention" principles (known by the acronym SCRAPES), all of which are assisted by dance/movement therapy intervention. These are: self-esteem and skill enrichment, conflict resolution and mediation skills, respect for differences, anger management and assertiveness training, problem solving skills, empathy training, and sexuality awareness training. How does dance/movement therapy address all of these? Through the constant reinforcement of body awareness, the acquisition of skill and achievement, the opportunity to learn how to adjust to others and oneself in time and space, and the sheer joy of moving—and through an adult's undivided positive attention.

When the California Department of Education had the funds and cared enough to use them, I worked with therapists to develop a workbook for teachers in special education settings. The workbook, which offered a set of skills and activities to be done with children in those settings, was entitled "I Can Do That!" I sincerely believe that this is the primary message we, as teachers of dance and as dance therapists, bring to children—and to adults. The *I* represents the ego, a person within and functioning; the *can do* is enabling and active in one's own behalf; the *that* is the mastery of skills; and the exclamation point is the mark of visibility—*See me!* What can be done is done, and shown, and shared. It is a positive demonstration of self, a very optimistic outcome to very hard work. Sometimes, it is achieved.

Perhaps the final word in exploring the world of creative dance and dance/ movement therapy is a quote from another dance pioneer, Barbara Mettler. In an article entitled "Dance—Art or Therapy?"[8] she concludes, "Therapists working with body movement need to know more about creative dance. Dancers working with sick people need to know more about therapy. Art and therapy overlap in practice, but it is important that workers in either field understand the differences between them."

To that, I would add, they might also recognize and respect the similarities: movement skill, craftsmanship, organization, respect for the body, its range, and limitations, the "mind-body connection," and above all, the creativity necessary to make both effective experiences for children and for the child who is forever within us. We go up and down, round and round, moving, inventing, and adapting the rich and complex world of dance and its potential for health and healing for children.[9]

NOTES

1. Harris Chaiklin, ed., *Marian Chace: Her Papers* (Columbia, MD: American Dance Therapy Association, 1975), 11.

2. See Marietta Eng, Maleta Boatman, and Joanna Gewertz-Harris, "The Occupational Therapy Program: A Creative Rhythmic Movement Group for Psychotic Children in a Psychotherapeutic Program," *Inpatient Care for the Psychotic Child* (Palo Alto, CA: Science and Behavior Books, 1971), 215. See also Joanna G. Harris, *A Practicum for Dance Therapy* (Berkeley, CA: Private printing, 1988), and Kathleen Criddle Mason, *Dance Therapy: Focus on Dance VII* (Washington, DC: American Alliance for Health, Physical Education, Recreation and Dance, 1974).

3. Judith Fried, "An Interview with Jane Manning," *American Journal of Dance Therapy* 17.1 (spring/summer 1995), 50.

4. Fran Levy, ed., *Dance and Other Expressive Art Therapies: When Words Are Not Enough* (New York: Routledge, 1995).

5. Fran Levy, ed., *Dance/Movement Therapy: A Healing Art* (Reston, VA: American Alliance for Health, Physical Education, Recreation and Dance, 1988), 229, 231–32.

6. Helen Payne, ed., *Dance/Movement Therapy: Theory and Practice* (London: Tavistock, 1992).

7. SuEllen Fried, "Bullies and Victims: Children Abusing Children," *American Journal of Dance Therapy* 18.2 (fall/winter, 1997), 132.

8. Barbara Mettler, "Dance—Art or Therapy," *American Journal of Dance Therapy* 12.2.

9. See also *American Journal of Dance Therapy* 11.2; 13.1; 16.1; 15.1–2.

19

Sharing the Gift of Dance: Ririe-Woodbury Dance Company's Bosnian Refugee Performances— Slovenia Tour, May 1993

JOAN J. WOODBURY

You're going where? Slovenia! Isn't that near Yugoslavia? Isn't that where all of the fighting is taking place? Will it be dangerous? Aren't you worried that someone will get hurt? These were just some of the questions asked by our friends when they discovered that the Ririe-Woodbury Dance Company had been invited to perform and teach in Ljubljana and Maribor.

It was very late in the season, almost the first of April, when we were able to say, "Yes, we can go." Negotiations to make this trip had been going on for over a year through the efforts of a wonderful Slovenian Olympic skier, Andreja Leskovsek-McQuarrie, who lives in Salt Lake City. Andreja's love for her homeland and the Ririe-Woodbury Dance Company made her want to bring the two together. What clinched the decision for us was a request that we perform for over five hundred Bosnian refugee children living in a collection center in Maribor, as well as a request to give a benefit concert in Celje to raise funds for the Bosnian refugees living in Slovenia. We felt a great sense of purpose and a strong desire to share the spirit of dance with people who had suffered so much. We made our plans to depart May 25, 1993—leaving only about a month to make all the necessary arrangements.

But leave we did—eight of us: Artistic Codirector Shirley Ririe, dancers Keith Johnson, Paul Callahan, Lisa Ford Moulton, Stephanie Nugent, and James Irvine, technical director Jeff Sturgis, and I. We flew to Munich, were picked up by two small Slovenian vans, and made the seven-hour drive to Ljubljana through the most breathtaking countryside. Little houses were tucked away in great green expanses of mountainous forest, beautiful stucco houses with tiled roofs that obviously had been built by people with a zest for life. The further south we went, the more gorgeous and quaint the country became. Nowhere did we see even the slightest indication that three hundred miles to the south a vicious war was raging. A strange unreality settled over all of us.

We arrived in Ljubljana enthusiastic to begin work. Teaching at the university was exciting and rewarding; students were eager, hungry, and talented, giving all they could every moment. To Shirley and me, it felt like the old days when we were all young, excited, a little naive, and nonjudgmental. There was spirit, commitment, and daring that one always wishes for in every class. The formal concert in Cankarjev Dom, Ljubljana, was also very well received, with vocal and lengthy audience responses.

Yet, I was waiting: waiting for a moment that I felt to be of great import, when we as artists could become part of a larger world picture. I know that dance speaks to the heart and the spirit, that through dance one can transcend. We were bringing art, not food, to a troubled people. I was silently waiting for the benefit concert in Celje and the performance in the collection center, which we were presenting for some of the seventy thousand Bosnian refugees living in Slovenia.

We arrived at the theater in Celje early the next afternoon. It was a jewel of a theater, with charming box seats surrounding the small main floor seating. It was over five hundred years old, we were told, and we could just imagine the royal dress that must have adorned those box seats. But the floor? Ten-inch-wide pine planks with the most gouges, holes, nails, cracks, and staples I had ever seen on a stage floor. And no vinyl dance flooring! An expression of terror fell over the faces of the dancers. Lively, emphatic discussions were held about the possibility of wearing sneakers, although everyone knew the dances we had selected would look ridiculous in shoes. So, they took a closer look at the floor and said, "We'll do it in bare feet." With great scrutiny, we got out the hammers and gaffers tape, and on hands and knees, prepared the dancing surface.

As curtain time neared, we were informed that many refugees were in the audience, along with townspeople who were there for financial support. We were pleased that Daniel Hall, cultural attaché from the American embassy, and Pauline Maurantonio, assistant to the American ambassador, had driven down from Ljubljana. Backstage came Father Kolsek, abbot for the north-central region of Slovenia, who had been asked to introduce our American modern dance company and to speak on the purpose of the evening's performance. Also invited to speak was Andrej Ster, chief secretary for public security, Republic of Slovenia Ministry of the Interior. We were all huddled in the small hallway between the stage and the dressing rooms, speaking energetically and all at once, half of us in English, half of us in Slovene, while unsuccessfully trying to make some sense out of what was being said and planned.

The evening seemed to rush by. The dancers were beautiful, radiant, and alive. Shirley and I were so proud of them. When the last dance ended, the audience didn't want to let us go. They clapped and clapped and clapped, not wanting the evening to end any more than we did. We danced an encore, and they applauded more. A wonderful energy flowed between us. The fatigue came afterwards.

Morning came early. The performance for the Bosnian children in the collection center was scheduled for 10:00 A.M., and our final formal concert in Maribor was scheduled that evening at 5:00. A full day. We were dropped off at the collection center at 9:00 A.M. I was surprised to find the center much as I had imagined it. The Bosnians were living in an old army barracks; a huge compound, probably one square city block, situated on a tree-lined street in the heart of the city. The barracks were brick stucco, painted a pinkish-yellowish tan. Posts of the same color and texture were widely spaced around the perimeter of the compound. Wire fencing between the posts formed the final boundary.

We were greeted instantly by children, lots of them, all neatly and cleanly dressed. They were curious and seemingly starved for affection and hope. We were told that five hundred children (persons sixteen years of age and younger) lived in the center and that it was extremely overcrowded. Women of all social strata, as evidenced by their clothes, were sweeping the asphalt sidewalks, while others simply watched our progress though the grassy center of the complex. Shyly, they began to collect around us, curiosity getting the better of them. We located the person making arrangements for the performance and began searching for a shady location large enough to accommodate both dancers and audience. The "stage" we chose in the end was a large, asphalt area next to some wooden benches and shaded by trees. The dancers would perform facing the oncoming sun, and as time passed, the small bower of shade was fast disappearing.

Preparations for our arrival had been good, if a bit casual. A van with a good sound system and microphone was being set up, while a CNN crew was going through the center photographing the refugees. We were preparing to start at 10:00 when we were informed that the time had been changed to 11:00 so that refugees from two other centers could come. I thought, "Wonderful, more people are coming," and at the same time, "The sun, the sun, the shade will be all gone."

We all busied ourselves with different things while we waited. I did "high-fives" with the children, going down the rows slapping hands and taking turns saying "Dober dan" and "Hello." The audience, adults and children alike, stayed very near the performing space, talking quietly to each other, watching the dancers warm up, chatting with them, and commenting about what they were seeing. A cameraman in our midst quietly took still pictures of the children, parents, and dancers together.

At this time, Shirley had been taken to a rest room in the complex, where she reported that today was cleaning day; women were washing clothes in small troughs and cleaning the rooms. Small army cubicles served as living quarters for four or five people, and everyone left their shoes outside the room so that they might keep their living spaces clean. There was no privacy for anyone at any time. When the army abandoned the barracks, it stripped the complex of all furniture. The townspeople of Maribor had furnished the refugees with mattresses, tables, chairs, and other basic living necessities.

We were told that the clothes the children wore were either those they arrived in, often their Sunday best, or those that had been given to them by a Slovenian family. The children wore these clothes in the heat and cold, day in and day out. Many of the children did not even know where their parents were or if they were alive. Many adults had the same questions about their children. They were living here as an extended family, clinging to each other and sharing in their common plight, hoping for a time when they could return to their homes or find new ones.

As 11:00 neared, more refugees arrived and walked casually into the audience area under the trees. The smaller children had been sitting on low stools in the front where they had waited for almost an hour. We were finally signaled to start. A gentleman from the complex introduced the company. Shirley and I had decided to take turns narrating the lecture demonstration with Andreja acting as an interpreter.

The performance was a joy from the outset. The dancers were introduced one by one as they leaped onto the stage. We chose dances that were funny, airy, spatial, and athletic, showing a wide range of qualities. The dancers looked wonderful in their tennis shoes and dark glasses, which they wore to protect them from the direct glare of the sun. The dances were soft, gentle, with women being wafted in the air, black tennis shoes on their feet. I laughed and cried.

To help everyone share in the motion and spirit of the dance, we always include audience participation in our informal performances. Language was no barrier. The audience was beautiful. As children were playing follow-the-leader with the dancers, a large woman began to scream. "Look, look. Look at her." She was pointing to a small, bare-armed girl who had joined the other children in the dance. The woman continued to scream and cry and then explained to Andreja that the child had been nearly catatonic ever since she arrived in the complex, barely moving and not speaking to anyone. And now she was dancing. People around the woman began to weep. We dancers knew this kind of phenomenon could happen because we had seen things like it before. But at this moment, with our desire to give something of ourselves to these people who so needed the joy that dance can bring, it was like a miracle.

As we ended, we invited everyone to join us on the asphalt area as we became sort of pied pipers, leading and encouraging everyone to dance with us. Waves of small, lean, wiggling bodies came forward, and we danced together in groups, all of us running, stopping, waving, leaning, singing, and turning, until the music thinned and finally stopped.

We then hugged and said our good-byes to this wonderful audience. But a good-bye is really a hello that sinks into your bones; I shall never forget the faces and the place and the feelings they brought. I received much more than I gave. We are all one world family and can do no more than share our humanity with each other. Dance was our gift to share.

Suggested Readings
Contributors

Suggested Readings

Anderson, Jack. *Art Without Boundaries*. Iowa City: University of Iowa Press, 1997.

Bartenieff, Irmgard, and Doris Lewis. *Body Movement: Coping with the Environment*. New York: Gordon and Breach, 1983.

Brown, Jean Morrison, ed. *The Vision of Modern Dance*. Princeton, NJ: Princeton Book, 1979.

Carter, Alexandra. *The Routledge Dance Studies Reader*. London: Routledge, 1998.

Chaiklin, Harris, ed. *Marian Chace: Her Papers*. Kensington, MD: American Dance Therapy Association, 1975.

Cohen, Marshall, and Roger Copeland, eds. *What Is Dance? Readings in Theory and Criticism*. Oxford: Oxford University Press, 1983.

Cohen, Selma Jean. *The Modern Dance (Seven Statements of Belief)*. Middletown, CT: Wesleyan University Press, 1966.

Conable, Barbara. *Marjorie Barstow: Her Teaching and Training*. Columbus, OH: Andover Road, 1989.

de Mille, Agnes. *The Book of Dance*. New York: Golden, 1963.

Dimondstein, Geraldine. *Children Dance in the Classroom*. New York: Macmillan, 1971.

Ellis, Havelock. *The Dance of Life*. Westport, CT: Greenwood, 1973.

Emery, Linne Fauley. *Black Dance in the United States from 1619 to 1970*. Palo Alto, CA: National Press Books, 1972.

Eng, Marietta, Maleta Boatman, and Joanna Gewertz-Harris. "The Occupational Therapy Program: A Creative Rhythmic Movement Group for Psychotic Children in a Psychotherapeutic Program." *Inpatient Care for the Psychotic Child*. Palo Alto, CA: Science and Behavior Books, 1971.

Feldenkrais, Moshe. *Awareness Through Movement*. New York: Harper and Row, 1972.

Fraleigh, Sondra Horton. *Dance and the Lived Body (A Descriptive Aesthetic)*. Pittsburgh: University of Pittsburgh Press, 1987.

Fraser, Diane Lynch. *Playdancing: Discovering and Developing Creativity in Young Children*. Pennington, NJ: Princeton Book, 1991.

Ghiselin, Brewster, ed. *The Creative Process*. Berkeley: University of California Press, 1952.

Halprin, Anna. *Moving Toward Life: Five Decades of Transformative Dance*. Ed. Rachel Kaplan. Middletown, CT: Wesleyan University Press, 1995.

Hawkins, Alma M. *Creating Through Dance*. Princeton, NJ: Princeton Book, 1983.

H'Doubler, Margaret. *Dance: A Creative Art Experience*. Madison: University of Wisconsin Press, 1998.

Highwater, Jamake. *Dance: Rituals of Experience*. New York: A & W, 1978.

Horosko, Marian. *Martha Graham: The Evolution of Her Dance Theory and Training, 1921–91*. Chicago: A Capella Books, 1991.

Horst, Louis, and Carroll Russell. *Modern Dance Forms in Relation to Other Modern Arts.* Princeton, NJ: Princeton Book, 1987.

Humphrey, Doris. *The Art of Making Dances.* New York: Rinehart, 1959.

Jayce, Mary. *Dance Technique for Children.* Palo Alto, CA: Mayfield Publishing, 1984.

Jones, Frank Pierce. *Body Awareness in Action: A Study of the Alexander Technique.* New York: Schocken Books, 1976.

Klosty, James. *Merce Cunningham.* New York: Limelight Editions, 1986.

Kostelanitz, Richard. *Merce Cunningham: Dancing in Space and Time.* Chicago: Chicago Review, 1992.

Lamb, Warren, and Elizabeth Watson. *Body Code: The Meaning in Movement.* Princeton, NJ: Princeton Book, 1987.

Langer, Susanne K. *Feeling and Form.* New York: Scribner, 1953.

——. *Problems of Art: Ten Philosophical Lectures.* New York: Scribner, 1957.

——, ed. *Reflections on Art: A Source Book of Writing by Artists, Critics and Philosophers.* New York: Arno, 1979.

Levy, Fran J., ed. *Dance and Other Expressive Art Therapies: When Words Are Not Enough.* New York: Routledge, 1995.

——. *Dance/Movement Therapy: A Healing Art.* Reston, VA: American Alliance for Health, Physical Education, Recreation and Dance, 1988.

Lloyd, Margaret. *The Borzoi Book of Modern Dance.* New York: Knopf, 1949.

Louis, Murray. *Inside Dance.* New York: St. Martin's Press, 1980.

——. *On Dance.* Chicago: A Capella Books, 1992.

Love, Paul. *Modern Dance Terminology.* Pennington, NJ: Princeton Book, 1997.

Martin, John. *Dance in Theory.* Princeton, NJ: Princeton Book, 1989.

——. *The Modern Dance.* New York: Barnes, 1933.

Mason, Kathleen Criddle. *Dance Therapy: Focus on Dance.* Vol. 7. Washington, DC: American Alliance for Health, Physical Education, Recreation and Dance, 1974.

Maynard, Olga. *American Modern Dancers (The Pioneers).* Boston: Little, Brown, 1965.

Mazo, Joseph H. *Prime Movers: The Makers of Modern Dance in America.* New York: Morrow, 1980.

Mendosa, Zoila. *Shaping Society Through Dance.* Chicago: University of Chicago Press, 2000.

Nagrin, Daniel. *Dance and the Specific Image (Improvisation).* Pittsburgh: University of Pittsburgh Press, 1994.

——. *How to Dance Forever (Surviving Against the Odds).* New York: Morrow, 1988.

Payne, Helen, ed. *Dance/Movement Therapy: Theory and Practice.* London: Tavistock, 1992.

Savio, Joanne, and Duane Cyrus. *Vital Grace: The Black Male Dancer.* Zurich: Edition Stemmle, 1999.

Sherbon, Elizabeth. *On the Count of One: Modern Dance Methods.* Palo Alto, CA: Mayfield, 1975.

Siegel, Marcia. *The Shapes of Change: Images of American Dance.* Boston: Houghton Mifflin, 1979.

Sorrell, Walter. *The Dance Has Many Faces.* Chicago: A Capella Books, 1992.

———. *Dance in Its Time.* New York: Columbia University Press, 1986.

———. *The Dancer's Image: Points and Counterpoints.* New York: Columbia University Press, 1971.

———. *The Dance Through the Ages.* New York: Grosset and Dunlap, 1967.

———, ed. *The Mary Wigman Book: Her Writings.* Middletown, CT: Wesleyan University Press, 1975.

Spolin, Viola. *Improvisation for the Theater.* Evanston, IL: Northwestern University Press, 1963.

Stanislavsky, Constantine. *Building a Character.* Trans. Elizabeth Reynolds Hapgood. Introduction by Joshua Logan. New York: Routledge, 1949.

———. *Creating a Role.* Ed. Hermine I. Popper. Trans. Elizabeth Reynolds Hapgood. New York: Routledge, 1989.

Sweigard, Lulu E. *Human Movement Potential (Its Ideokinetic Facilitation).* Lanham, MD: University Press of America, 1988.

Turner, Margery I. *New Dance.* Pittsburgh, PA: University of Pittsburgh Press, 1971.

Wigman, Mary. *The Language of Dance.* Trans. Walter Sorrell. Middletown, CT: Wesleyan University Press, 1966.

Contributors

BECKY ENGLER-HICKS is a registered dance-movement therapist and psychotherapist in private practice in St. Louis and Santa Barbara. She is the founder and director of Kinder Bright Infant Learning. Currently, she is finishing her PhD in prenatal and perinatal psychology.

RUTH GRAUERT served as stage manager for the Nikolais Dance Theater and the Murray Louis Dance Company and as lighting director for the Phyllis Lamhut and the Beverly Blossom dance companies, Washington University Dance Theater, and others. She is the director of Bearnstow, an arts camp for children and adults in Maine. She writes and lectures on dance and current culture, teaches dance lighting and creative writing, and is the editor of the *Journal of Art and Idea,* a Web site magazine.

ANNA HALPRIN, PhD, a pioneer in dance and theater, has influenced the principal theater and dance centers of the world. She is the cofounder of the Tamalpa Institute, a movement-based expressive arts educational center, and the author of five books. Besides numerous honors, she has received the Lifetime Achievement Award in dance from the American Dance Festival.

JOANNA G. HARRIS, PhD, ADTR, a pioneer dance therapist and Fulbright scholar, trained at the University of Wisconsin, Mills College, and the University of California, Berkeley. She founded the Creative Arts Therapy Graduate Program at Lone Mountain College and Antioch College in San Francisco. She is the author of *A Practicum for Dance Therapy* and the coeditor of the *American Journal of Dance Therapy* and is currently an adjunct faculty member of the Center for Psychological Studies (Albany, California) and the Modern Dance Center (Berkeley).

MARGARET N. H'DOUBLER was a professor of dance at the University of Wisconsin–Madison, where she taught for forty-four years. In 1926, she established the first dance major in the country and through her teaching has profoundly influenced the way dance is taught in schools and universities today. She wrote four books and received numerous honors, including the 1964 Dance Magazine Award.

MICHAEL HOEYE is a novelist and the creator of *The Adventures of Hermux Tantamoq*. He has also been a photographer, a painter, a choreographer, and an advertising copywriter. He received his BA from Washington University in the 1960s, where he studied with Annelise Mertz. In 1989, he completed graduate work in psychiatry and religion at Union Theological Seminary in New York. From 1992 to 1998, he developed and taught the Innovation and Creativity curriculum in the MBA program at Maryhurst University in Portland, Oregon.

MURRAY LOUIS has been a dancer, a choreographer, a teacher, a videographer, and an author during the course of a fifty-year career. The artistic director of the Murray Louis and Nikolais Dance Company, he is currently involved in preparing both the extensive archives of Nikolais and Louis for the University of Ohio and a national and international tour for his company. Besides numerous awards, he has received honorary degrees from the University of Ohio and Rutgers University. He has authored two books, *Inside Dance* and *On Dance*.

ANNELISE MERTZ, a dancer, a teacher, and a choreographer, is a professor emerita of dance at Washington University. She is the founder and former director of the university's dance division, its Dance Theater (a student-faculty performance group), and the St. Louis Dancers (a professional company). She also founded Dance St. Louis, an organization that presents professional dance companies from all over the world. A native of Berlin, Germany, she has performed extensively throughout Europe with the Jooss Tanztheater, the Berlin State Opera, and several municipal operas. She has also taught nationally and internationally. Among the awards she has received as a teacher and choreographer are the Excellence in the Arts Award from the Arts and Education Council of Greater St. Louis and the YWCA Art Leadership Award. In March 2001, Washington University named its dance studio at the Edison Theater after her.

JAIME NISENBAUM, MA, REAT, holds a master's degree in psychology and is a registered expressive arts therapist. He trained in somatic and Gestalt therapy with Robert K. Hall and in expressive arts therapy with Daria Halprin. He is the codirector of the Tamalpa Institute, an adjunct faculty member in the Expressive Arts Program at the California Institute of Integral Studies, and a lecturer in several universities. He maintains a private practice in Marin County, California.

CAROL NORTH joined Metro Theater Company in 1977 as a performer. She toured with the company for ten years, assuming artistic leadership of the organization in 1980. The recipient of the 1995 St. Louis YWCA Art Leadership Award and the 1998 Excellence in the Arts Award from the Arts and Education Council of Greater St. Louis, she is an adjunct instructor at Maryville University in St. Louis.

JEFF REHG received a BA in recreation administration from California State University–Chico. He was camp director for Trail Blazer Camps in New York, which provided disadvantaged inner-city children with a twenty-six-day wilderness experience; head counselor of a Berkeley, California, group home for emotionally disturbed teens; and the program director of child care for the Berkeley-Albany YMCA.

SHIRLEY RIRIE cofounded the Ririe-Woodbury Dance Company in 1964 and since then has been its artistic codirector. She was also a Fulbright professor in Hong Kong and New Zealand. She choreographed numerous works for her own and for other professional dance companies. She began teaching at the University of Utah in 1955, retiring as a full professor in 1995. She has received numerous awards, including the 1980 Distinguished Woman of the Year Award from the University of Utah, the Honors in the Arts Award from the Salt Lake City Chamber of Commerce in 1982, the Plaudit Award in 1981 from the National Dance Association, and an honorary doctorate from the University of Utah in 1999.

EMMA D. SHEEHY taught at Columbia University's Teachers College and was the author of several books, including *Children Discover Music and Dance* and *The 5's and 6's Go to School*.

G. HOFFMAN SOTO is an eclectic movement artist with over thirty years of study, practice, and teaching, including a long association with Anna Halprin. He utilizes many of the postmodern dance styles, including Butoh, movement theater, and movement awareness, as well as African and Brazilian dance, in his teaching. He has been a student of the martial arts for more than three decades and has performed and taught internationally since 1979 in Europe, Canada, Japan, Australia, and the Middle East. He teaches in the San Francisco Bay area at the Tamalpa Institute, the New College of California, and the Alive and Well Institute of Conscious Body Work.

HAROLD TAYLOR, as the president of Sarah Lawrence College, pioneered new scholastic methods for fourteen years until he resigned to devote himself entirely to teaching and writing. He is a spokesperson for art education and has a profound understanding of the creative process, its significance in daily life, and its importance to the cultural problems of our time.

BRANISLAV TOMICH has performed at the Kennedy Center for the Performing Arts, Carnegie Hall, the Brooklyn Academy of Music, and theaters, universities, and museums throughout the country. He has appeared on public television and in sitcoms and independent films. His work as a solo theater artist has been honored by the National Endowment for the Arts and by a 1994 Los Angeles DramaLogue Award for *Cafe God*, an existential comedy.

DOROTHY M. VISLOCKY, a professor emerita at Hunter College of the City University of New York, conceived and developed the curriculum for the dance major program, emphasizing creative aspects of choreographing and performing. She directed the program from 1972 to 1986 and currently teaches courses in the creative process and in anatomy and kinesiology. An original member of the Alwin Nikolais Dance Company from 1952 to 1962, she choreographed and directed for the Dorothy Vislocky Dance Theater from 1963 to 1984.

JOAN J. WOODBURY is a graduate of the University of Wisconsin and was the first Fulbright scholar in dance at the Freie Universität in Berlin, Germany, where she studied with Mary Wigman. She was a professor of modern dance at the University of Utah from 1951 to 1998. She is a cofounder and artistic director of the Ririe-Woodbury Dance Company, for which she has choreographed extensively. She has received several awards for her work as a choreographer and a teacher, as well as honorary doctorates from Southern Utah University in 1989 and from the University of Utah in 1999.

CREDITS FOR CONTRIBUTORS' PHOTOS

Becky Engler-Hicks with a student from her "Baby Bright" class. Printed
with permission from Becky Engler-Hicks.

Ruth Grauert. Photograph by Nan Melville; printed with permission from
the Nikolais-Louis Foundation for Dance.

Anna Halprin. Photograph by Coni Beeson; printed with permission from
Anna Halprin.

Joanna G. Harris. Photograph printed with permission from Joanna G.
Harris.

Michael Hoeye. Photograph by Martha Banyas; printed with permission
from Michael Hoeye.

Murray Louis. Photograph by Nan Melville; printed with permission from
the Nikolais-Louis Foundation for Dance.

Annelise Mertz. Photograph by Washington University Photographic Service.

Jaime Nisenbaum. Photograph by James B. Wood; printed with permission
from Jaime Nisenbaum.

Carol North. Photograph by J. Bruce Summers; printed with permission
from Carol North.

Shirley Ririe. Photograph by Virginia Robinson; printed with permission
from Shirley Ririe.

G. Hoffman Soto. Photograph printed with permission from G. Hoffman
Soto.

Branislav Tomich. Photograph by Eric Vigil; printed with permission from
Branislav Tomich.

Dorothy M. Vislocky. Photograph by Arthur Elgort; printed with permission
from Dorothy M. Vislocky.

Joan J. Woodbury. Photograph printed with permission from Joan J.
Woodbury.